Flying High With A Frank Steward

More Air Travel Tips and Tales From the Flight Crew

Also by James Wysong

- *Air Travel Tales From the Flight Crew*
- *The Plane Truth*
- *The Air Traveler's Survival Guide*

Flying High With A Frank Steward

More Air Travel Tips and Tales From the Flight Crew

JAMES WYSONG

(AKA A. FRANK STEWARD)

Impact Publications
Manassas Park, VA

Flying High with A Frank Steward

ISBN: 1-57023-272-5
        978-1-57023-272-5

Library of Congress: 2005929762

Photo Credit: Photograph on back cover courtesy of Tyler Mallory.

Publisher: For information on Impact Publications, including current and forthcoming publications, authors, press kits, online bookstore, and submissions, visit our website: www.impactpublications.com

Publicity/Rights: For information on publicity, author interviews, and subsidiary rights, contact Media Relations Department: Tel. 703-361-7300, Fax 703-335-9486, or e-mail: info@impactpublications.com.

Sales/Distribution: All bookstore sales are handled through Impact's trade distributor: National Book Network, 15200 NBN Way, Blue Ridge Summit, PA 17214, Tel. 1-800-462-6420. All other sales and distribution inquiries should be directed to the publisher: Sales Department, IMPACT PUBLICATIONS, 9104 Manassas Drive, Suite N, Manassas Park, VA 20111-5211, Tel. 703-361-7300, Fax 703-335-9486, or e-mail: info@impactpublications.com

Acknowledgments

This book would not have been possible if it weren't for my editor, dear friend, and plane folk "father" Robert Younglof, to whom I am most grateful.

I would like to thank my wife Toni and my son Oliver for making it all worthwhile. I would also like to thank MSNBC.com and Tripso.com for featuring my weekly column and giving me the outlet to display these writing urges. I would like to thank my Tripso column editor Nancy Zerby for her invaluable help and tolerance with my deadline discretions.

But in the end, I want to thank you, the passenger, crewmember, or interesting fellow traveler, who make my life more rewarding and help keep my journey a true joy for me.

Foreword

The journey, not the destination, is the true joy. I know it may sound like an old bumper sticker, but this saying holds a lot of truth and meaning to me. I have been a flight attendant for a major American international airline for the past 20 years and have had a front row ticket to one of the greatest shows on earth that I would like to share with you.

My other favorite saying is, *He who laughs, lasts.* Because life is too short not to appreciate all the humor involved, especially when it comes to air travel. If we look closely into the world of commercial flying, we will find that air travel and all the characters encountered provide fascinating insights into the boundless variations that make up human nature.

Combine these two sayings and you have the theme of my book, for my job onboard is part of your journey. For two decades, I have served, witnessed, and written about the hysterical antics of air travel, the bizarre behavior of passengers and crewmembers, and travel mistakes that are made over and over. In this book, I offer many tips that can help you with your flying experience from start to finish, supply you with entertainment and laughter, and maybe serve as a travel companion no matter where you are heading.

We dedicate so much time in the planning and preparation of our leisure and business trips, but virtually no time or thought into the actual journey itself. Hopefully, that is something this book can change.

If you agree, disagree, like, or dislike what I say, or have a tip or a story that you want to share, feel free to e-mail me at <u>Afranksteward@aol. com</u>. I represent no one specific airline, but you may see certain similarities on every airline you fly. This book is essentially a collection of my columns at <u>tripso.com</u> and <u>msnbc.com</u>. So, if you have followed them routinely, you might be familiar with some of these chapters. At times, I may repeat and contradict myself, and you may not always agree with everything that I have to say, but if you can use some of the tips offered, it may be worth more than any upgrade.

Now, I invite you to sit back, relax, and really start to enjoy your journey!

Contents

PART ONE

In the Terminal

CHAPTER ONE

Choose Your Airline Wisely

I t seems that after every flight, some passenger will vow never to fly with my airline again. Invariably, someone else on that flight will declare us the best carrier in the sky. So what makes a good airline? And how do you choose?

With all the recent fare wars, bankruptcy filings, and job actions, the question becomes even more complicated. Is ticket price the most important factor? What about destinations, flight frequency, and customer service? There are so many things to consider.

But wait. Let's narrow things down. Here are some sure signs that an airline should not make your short list.

1. The fuselage is patched up with duct tape.

2. You have to be a contortionist to get into your seat.

3. The airline's CEO makes a gazillion dollars, yet the company is facing bankruptcy.

4. The airline guarantees your luggage will "get there too," or it will refund your low-fare ticket price. (I don't know about you, but I would much rather have my bags than $29.)

5. The airline offers charter flights to nudists. (Eeew!)

Okay. Time to get serious. Choosing an airline needn't be nerve-racking. Just keep these 10 points in mind:

1. **Shop around.** Before settling in with one airline, fly several different ones first. And remember: You're not locked into one airline just because you're in its mileage club. You can be a member of many different clubs.

2. **Make reservations.** Call each airline's customer service line and see if you get through promptly. Do this at several different times of day over the course of a week. If you keep getting busy signals, think about how you would feel if you really needed some help.

3. **Check the gate.** If there is only one gate agent for a full 747 flight, be suspicious. This is probably a sign that manpower is stretched on the airplane, in customer service, and possibly on the maintenance crew as well.

4. **Check the seats.** Sure, it's great to stretch out on an uncrowded flight, but too many empty seats should make you wonder about the airline's profitability. If layoffs are coming, that roomy comfort won't last.

5. **Check the extras.** When choosing an airline, you don't want a fixer-upper. If on-board amenities such as reading lights, the entertainment system, and lavatories are in good condition, chances are the engines and electronics have been well maintained, too.

6. **Altitude attitude.** Times are tough for just about everyone in the airline industry, and often there's little to smile about. So when you encounter pleasant employees, chances are the airline is treat-

ing them in a fair and equitable manner, which bodes well for its long-term stability.

7. **Shell out some cash.** If you are presented with a choice of airlines and the fare difference is small, don't be cheap. Go with the one that has served you best in the past. The $20 you save with the cheaper airline will disappear fast if you have to wait out a delay in the airport bar.

8. **Join the club.** If you're on business and the company is paying, then pay close attention to the airline's frequent-flier mileage scheme. The terms and conditions are often complex, but knowledge pays off in upgrades and perks.

9. **Numbers don't lie.** Pay no attention to accolades. Most of the praise comes from airline shills posing as media. ("Voted best airline." Yeah, right—by its own shareholders, maybe.) Instead, ask the airline for some numbers, paying particular attention to on-time rates, flight frequency, and recent layoffs.

10. **Safety first.** As a flight attendant, I think an airline's safety record and fleet age (the average age of its airplanes) should be your concern, but these are factors that passengers often overlook. Fortunately, this is public information, and you can get most airlines' safety records online: www.faa.gov or www.ntsb.gov.

It is important to understand that most of the big airlines are in fact very similar. Whatever one does, the other soon hears about and tries to copy. If Joe's Airline starts handing out lemon-scented armpit fresheners, then Ed's Airways will eventually offer the same. You should also remember that every carrier will have both good and bad flights, along with good and bad crews.

In the end, it comes down to your own needs and experiences. Shop around, compare carefully, and you will fly happily.

CHAPTER TWO

Pet Peeves About Air Travel

L et's face it, when it comes to air travel, some things are done in an intelligent manner, and some things are handled stupidly. This chapter deals with the latter.

I once wrote a column called *"12 Ridiculous Things about Air Travel"* and asked readers to send me their own contributions to the list. Here are the results: a varied collection of pet peeves and wry observations —along with some polite disagreements and a handful of explanations. Many thanks to the contributors, who shall remain anonymous.

The Biggest Gripes

1. **"Seatback in the upright position."** Scores of people asked, "Is a lousy two-inch pitch really going to make much of a difference during takeoff and landing?" (See answer, below.)

2. **Security.** My original column came at the height of the London bomb scare, unleashing a torrent of complaints about the new no-liquids policy and the goons rifling through your bags. And why, people asked, can duty-free shops continue to sell items that their clueless customers cannot take on the airplane?

3. **In-flight "snacks."** "Why bother to give out half-ounce packages?" asked one reader. "I counted, and there were only eight peanuts in a package. I saved mine so as not to spoil my dinner that night."

4. **Electronic equipment.** If studies have shown that battery-powered devices do not, in fact, interfere with the cockpit instruments, why do the airlines continue to prohibit them?

5. **Boarding procedures.** I hit a nerve when I counted boarding procedures among the top 12 ridiculous things about air travel. Hundreds of complaints about this one—many travelers feel that the airlines are doing everything possible to complicate a simple procedure.

6. **Seat cushions.** While praising the seat cushion for its services as a "rear-end comforter and fart sponge," one reader remained skeptical about its suitability as a flotation device. "Come on," the reader said, "how many people who are bobbing up and down after crashing in the water say, 'Hey, I will grab onto the floating seat cushion'?"

7. **Legroom.** Much derision over the often-heard announcement that your primary stowage area is under the seat in front of you. "It may be true if you didn't have any legs," scoffed one reader, "but don't insult us with that kind of foolishness."

8. **Carry-ons.** There were many complaints that carry-on luggage is not subject to a weight limit. As one reader put it, "So the moron who boards with two rollerboards, a briefcase, and a laptop gets away with delaying the flight and making us all feel like strangling him."

9. **Reservations.** Have you tried to get hold of a reservations agent lately? No? Here's what to expect: a busy signal, a long wait on hold, or a computer "helper" that constantly misinterprets your request. If you finally get hold of a person, he or she will hail from

some country you have never heard of and will understand only 50 percent of your conversation.

10. **Outsource what?** Okay, I realize that the trend in American business is to outsource as much work as possible to foreign workforces. But I think outsourcing aircraft repair and maintenance is going too far.

11. **Charge!** Okay, charge extra for an alcoholic drink, maybe a meal and a headset, but keep things within reason. Some airlines are now charging for aisle or window seats, soft drinks, and even water. What's next? Overhead bin space and coin-operated lavatories?

12. **Luggage stores.** Why are there luggage stores at the airport? I think you can assume that if travelers have made it that far, their luggage needs have been properly satisfied.

13. **No Smoking signs.** I'm pretty sure everyone knows that smoking is not allowed on-board and never will be again. So why are there illuminated signs above every seat and ashtrays all over the airplane?

My Favorite Pet Peeves From Readers

Readers had countless pet peeves and recitals of personal bad luck at airports, in security lines, on the plane, and at the baggage carousel. Here are some of my favorites, in the readers' own words.

1. **No nuts.** "I have noticed the airlines now serve pretzels that are tough as nails and taste like cardboard. Are they cheaper or just afraid of lawsuits from medical incidents? My wife is allergic to peanuts and she knows very well not to eat them. The airlines should just serve the nuts, or at least grow a couple."

2. **End points.** "Why do we have to arrive and depart from a place called a 'terminal'?"

3. **Pilots' dinner.** "Suppose you're on a flight that has no hot food on-board, and the flight attendant carries a hot crew meal for the pilots up from the back and the smell wafts through the cabin. Is

that a tease? If the passengers don't get hot meals, neither should the crew, or at least be more discreet!"

4. **On and off.** "If they are going to preboard passengers with special needs, shouldn't they be the last ones off instead of struggling with their bags and holding up the rest of the passengers?"

5. **Bathroom runs.** "In this day and age, when you have to arrive at the airport several hours before a flight, and sit around the waiting area for half that time, why, oh why, must several people always have to clog the aisles to use the bathroom while the plane is still boarding?"

6. **Clutter in the seat pockets.** "Does anyone actually buy anything from SkyMall? Has anyone ever taken the complimentary inflight magazine home with them for the engrossing articles ('*Five Best Things to Do in Des Moines*')?"

7. **Security, obviously.** "Have you looked at the TSA website lately? They do not list whether you can bring iPods or MP3 players on a plane (something that about 50 percent of travelers have), but they take pains to list that you cannot take cattle prods, ninja throwing stars, or nunchuks. DUH!"

Five Things That Seem Ridiculous, But Actually Do Have a Reason

Finally, here are five seemingly senseless things that actually do have a reason. Some of these I just learned myself.

1. Life vest instructions on land flights. Lots of people asked, "Why bother?" Answer: It is for consistency and in case the flight gets diverted. The FAA's policy is to be ready for all contingencies on every flight.

2. Doesn't everyone know how to operate a seat belt by now? Probably. So why bother with the tedious seat belt instructions? Answer: This was the leadoff complaint in my original column, and I have since been set straight. The thinking is that passengers who

are reminded about the seat belt at the beginning of a flight are more apt to remember it during an emergency, when common sense loses its grip.

3. "Seatback in the upright position." I promised you an answer on this one and here it is. Yes, the extra five degrees of lean does make a difference in an emergency. The FAA has proven that it takes 15 to 45 seconds longer to evacuate an airplane when the seats are reclined. Each of those seconds could be a life lost.

4. Shades up on takeoff and landing. "Why?" a reader asked. "Sometimes I think the flight attendants are just on a power trip. Here I am, pupils scorched by the sunlight, desperate to get some shut-eye, and I have a flight attendant yelling at me to put the shade up." Answer: In an emergency you will need to have the shades up so you can see what is happening outside the aircraft.

5. "Who packed your luggage?" This security question landed some sarcastic remarks, like, "Does anybody ever say that it was packed by an angry gentleman of apparently Middle Eastern origin mumbling something about 'death to all crusaders'?" Answer: Well, no. But the question might get you thinking about that "gift" that your roommate's uncle asked you to carry for him to New York.

A couple of readers complained that I refer to air travel as a joke when it should be considered serious business. While I don't want to be sitting next to these readers on a long flight, I do appreciate their opinion. In fact, I do think of air travel as a joke, the same way I look on all of life as a humorous journey. For me, seeing the humor in every situation is a good way to keep sane. On the other hand, my wife says I'm not all that sane anyway, so maybe the serious folks are right after all.

CHAPTER THREE

Airport: The Cast of Characters

L et's take a look at some of the characters you might encounter as you make your way through your airplane trip.

1. **The Lady of the Keyboard.** This is the ticket agent who appears to be typing a novel—and faster than any typist you have ever seen. After a while, she starts talking to her screen as if she has an ongoing relationship with it. Just when you think the system has lost your booking, the computer spits out baggage tags, boarding cards, and itineraries, but before you can say thank you, the gate agent is on to the next customer.

2. **The Security Tag Team.** The one out front talks as if he has had way too much coffee, yammering about metal objects, laptops,

and liquids; the other one, behind the monitor, looks dazed and about to doze off, like a couch potato glued to the television set.

3. **The Berated Gate Agent.** This poor woman has heard every upgrade ploy and excuse for an aisle seat known to man. She rarely makes eye contact, knits her brow a lot, and appears to be contemplating serious matters. What she is really thinking about is how wonderful her life will be when your airplane doors are finally closed.

4. **The Condescending Flight Attendant.** This employee has developed a bitter attitude over time and treats all passengers as if their only goal in life is to make her miserable. She assumes you're an idiot and treats you like one.

5. **Biff and Bruce.** These fellows represent the two extremes of behavior among male flight attendants. Biff rolls up his sleeves, sticks his chest out, and tells macho jokes to prove to everyone that he is not gay. Bruce, on the other hand, is so effeminate that he practically floats through the aisles.

6. **Ms. Don't-Mess-with-Me.** This flight attendant, who seems to have come aboard fresh from a fight with her better half, answers the first passenger complaint with a glare that unmistakably says, "Make my day—one word from me and the cops will handcuff you." Good thing she's not carrying a gun.

7. **The Strong, Silent Pilot.** Airline pilots are generally uncommunicative and given to stretching the truth. There are some who feel no need to tell their passengers anything about why the airplane has yet to leave the gate or why it has been sitting on the runway for three hours. Others tell small, folksy lies: "OK, folks, keep those seat belts on. We should be at the gate in just a couple of minutes." It is interesting that these pilots can fly complex instrument approach routes but can't estimate time worth a damn.

8. **The Garrulous Pilot.** This pilot wants to talk you across the Atlantic Ocean. Forget the sleep you were going to get on-board, because this guy is going to point out every whitecap along the way. Spare me! If it was the ocean 10 minutes ago, I can assume

that it is the same body of water now. And if these chatty pilots are going to constantly talk over the loud speaker, shouldn't they have to take a speech class to eliminate all the long, drawn-out "*Uuuuuuuhhhhhhh's*"?

9. **Ms. Welcome Wagon.** This is the ground agent who welcomes you and announces your baggage-claim area. Why does this person always have such a strong accent? Half the time I can't understand where I've landed. Shouldn't the one welcoming you to the United States have a firm grip on the English language?

10. **The Unflappable Customer Service Agent.** This is the one you go to when your flight has canceled and you need to be rerouted. He's heard it all—from how you "can't believe this is happening" and how your trip "has been totally ruined" to how you are "never going to fly with this airline again." The fact that the agent remains completely unfazed gets you riled up even more.

11. **The Burly Baggage Guys.** You see these big, capable-looking fellows when you look out the airplane window during boarding. Your equanimity is shaken as you see them hurling the suitcases onto the moving ramp with enthusiasm, probably exploding all the liquids and gels you were forced to pack in your checked-in luggage.

12. **The Sticky Maintenance Crew.** These guys come on-board to fix a last-minute problem, armed with stickers that say "Inoperative" or "Deferred," ready to slap them on anything that's not crucial to flight safety. The idea seems to be: If it's broken, don't fix it. Just put a sticker on it.

13. **The Smiley Faces.** Then there are the flight attendants who have not cracked a smile the entire flight, but manage to flash a drop-dead-gorgeous smile as they utter their monotonous "Buh-bye!" to each and every one of the passengers.

14. **What kind of character am I?** I'm the flight attendant who tells you exactly what I'm thinking—quite candidly—but I do it in a humorous tone of voice. For example, "Four carry-on bags? Where's the kitchen sink?" So instead of getting angry, you just chuckle and get annoyed later.

CHAPTER FOUR

Terror Plot: Cancel Your Flight?

I have received countless e-mails and phone calls from people asking whether they should cancel their upcoming flight plans to Europe. Concerns about the latest London terrorism plot—and hassles at security—have certainly cast a pall on that stroll down the Champs d'Elysée and that double-decker bus ride through Trafalgar Square.

It is true that the extra security procedures are frustrating and time-consuming, but with all the safety checks, it is actually safer to fly now than ever. The Transportation Security Administration (TSA) is on full alert and the chances of anyone or anything getting past its scrutiny now are slim. Experienced fliers know this. In fact, airline employees tend to make their own flight plans after industry scares like this. We know that the media will overplay the fear card, passengers will cancel, and there will be plenty of seats for flying standby.

Me, I've traded out of a working trip to California and went to London instead—partly because I needed some time off, but mostly because I wanted to see what it's like to fly aboard a jumbo aircraft with the overhead bins almost completely empty. As you may know, carry-on luggage was extremely limited on all flights to England. It was a sight that I just couldn't miss.

I have a love-hate relationship with England. I was based there with Pan Am, met the woman of my dreams at Heathrow Airport, finished my degree at London University, and made quite a few friends in the pubs. I have fond memories of my 10-year British exile, but also some bad ones. I lost a couple of friends in Lockerbie 103; I was disrupted by the frequent terrorist attacks of the Irish Republican Army; and my then-pregnant wife and I missed the London bombings last summer by just one day (we used the very Tube station that was blown up 24 hours later). Terrorism is no stranger to that country, but things will return to normal before long.

The thing to remember is that this most recent terrorist plot was in fact spoiled, and the expertise of the authorities has prevented another. Sadly, this won't be the last incident. Terrorism will be a way of life for all of us for a long time to come.

Keeping all this in mind, here are some tips if you decide to fly:

1. **Show up early.** The new security procedures are extensive and somewhat tedious, and it will take you longer than usual to clear.

2. **Keep informed.** Call your airline the night before your flight for up-to-the-minute information, or go to www.tsa.gov for the latest security information. Certain items may be prohibited one day, but allowed the next.

3. **Stay dry.** Pack all your liquids, gels, perfumes over three ounces—anything that can be shaken or stirred—into your checked luggage. If you're not one to check baggage, it's time to start.

4. **Exceptions.** So far, the main exceptions to the no-liquids rule are prescription medications (up to four ounces accompanied by the doctor's prescription) and baby food (you might be required to taste it in front of the TSA agent, so bring your favorite flavor).

5. **Be reasonably suspicious.** If you see other passengers acting suspiciously, get a second opinion before reporting them to authorities. Remember that every passenger you see, including you, has gone through security procedures at the highest level.

6. **Be patient.** TSA personnel don't like going through your bags picking out prohibited items any more than you do. It's not like the security screeners smell better and look cleaner now that they're confiscating your toiletries. They are just doing their jobs.

Bottom line: Go ahead with your flight plans. In fact, relax and enjoy—not because *"If I don't go, the terrorists will win,"* but because you can count on security making air travel safer than it ever has been. You've looked forward to your trip, and it would be a shame to call it off.

If you're going to London, enjoy your trip through Trafalgar Square. And, hey, if you see me at a pub, I'll buy you your first pint.

CHAPTER FIVE

Getting Bumped? Make It Pay

Airlines say they are in business to get you safely from one place to another. But let's face it: They're in it for the money. That's why, when you show up for your flight, the gate agent sometimes asks for volunteers to take a later flight. It's called a bump. What happens next is called a bribe, and it can pay off very nicely—in tickets, upgrades, and/or cold, hard cash.

Why do airlines oversell flights? Because passengers have an average no-show rate of about 15 percent. Say an airline booked only 300 passengers for a 300-seat flight to Europe. On average, 45 of those passengers would fail to show up. The airplane would still go to Europe, but 45 seats would be empty. The no-shows get their money back, so the airline loses the revenue from those 45 seats, which digs deep into the company's profit margin. So the airline overbooks the flight. In a sense, the airline is depending on the passengers to be 15 percent unreliable.

It's when everybody shows up that it starts getting interesting. To persuade some of those passengers to take another flight, the gate agents offer bribes. Typically, the offer will include an upgrade on the next flight, a $400 flight coupon good for travel anywhere the airline flies, and hotel accommodations, if needed.

Tempting? Sure. Still, passengers usually scoff at the offer, because they've got to be where they've got to be, and when they've got to be there. If the airline doesn't get enough volunteers on the first call, the offer goes up. I have seen the offer rise to $1,200 cash plus a first-class ticket on any flight on our airline. It's a game, and anyone can play.

One late-August afternoon, I met a passenger who played the game very well. Stanley was waiting for the same flight that I was. Unfortunately, the flight was full, and since I was a pass rider (an airline employee on standby), there was no way I was going to get on. I was frustrated, but when the call was made for volunteers to take another flight, Stanley's face lit up in a smile.

"Why are you so pleased?" I inquired.

"Well, as the offer goes up, so does my price," he chuckled.

"I don't follow you."

"Well, I have volunteered already, and this makes three days in a row."

No wonder Stanley was pleased. Over three days of bumped flights, he had raked in $2,200 worth of flight coupons, three free nights in a lovely hotel in a great city, free meal vouchers, four free 15-minute long-distance phone calls, and an upgrade on the next flight he gets on (if he gets on). He said it happened every year, and that this was the third year in a row that he was doing "the bump thing," as he put it. One year he collected more than $8,000 and finally ended up with a ticket refund after more than a week of being bumped from one flight to another.

The "bump thing" works for Stanley because he is flexible. He has his own business, and he plans his vacation for the same time and same flight every year. While he does have things to do when he finally arrives at his destination, he also gets a lot of work done on his laptop while hanging around the airport. Meanwhile, he usually manages to collect his company's travel money for the year.

Stanley knew I was a pass rider, so he offered me a place to sleep that night. Considering that there wasn't going to be a vacant room in the city, I took him up on it. He had bet the hotel manager that he would be back, and his prize was a suite, so there was plenty of room for me.

We ate and drank on the airline's meal voucher and tried again the next day. When the familiar announcement came over the PA system, Stanley started chuckling again. I bade him farewell, as I had to find some way to get back to work that day.

Stanley's game is perfectly legal, ethical, moral, and fair. The airlines don't care how many times you volunteer; they just want to free up those seats. So if you hear that call for volunteers and can afford the time, go for it. There are lots of rewards, and who knows—it could lead to serendipitous adventures.

Here are some tips to remember when bumping your way to cheap travel.

1. **Pay attention.** If you volunteer your seat and the price of the bribe later goes up, make sure you get the top price as well.

2. **Get it in writing.** If the airline promises you travel credit, an upgrade, dinner—or anything else—have the agent write down the offer and sign it with her employee number. Finding the same gate agent again may be difficult. If you don't have proof of the offer, you could miss out.

3. **Ask for more.** When the agent rebooks your flight, ask for an upgrade. Many times, there will be no problem granting the request. If the airline can't deliver on the upgrade at the time of the flight, get some type of travel credit or compensation for that as well.

4. **Have a good night.** If your new flight schedule requires a night stay, the airline must provide hotel accommodation. Make sure you get a hotel with adequate airport transportation, or get a taxi voucher.

5. **Waste time wisely.** If the airline books you on a flight requiring more than a two-hour wait in the airport, ask for permission to use its club lounge. Here you will find such amenities as free drinks, snacks, television, and computer workstations.

6. **Do it all again.** If your rebooked flight is also oversold, go ahead and give up your seat again.

Denied boarding situations happen anytime there is an oversold flight, but in my experience, they are most likely to occur during major holidays, spring break, and at the beginning and end of summer. Stanley mentioned August 29 to September 7 as prime bumping season.

CHAPTER SIX

How to Save a Canned Flight

I f this book were an airline, what would you be hearing right now?

"Ladies and gentlemen, this chapter is running behind schedule due to a late inbound column. I apologize for the delay but it shouldn't be more than 15 minutes."

Or maybe ...

"Attention in reading area: the chapter has arrived but is experiencing mechanical difficulties; we have an editor on-board working on the problem. The problem should not take longer than about 30 minutes."

Or, perhaps ...

"I am sorry to announce that the author has run out of legalities for today, so we will have to cancel this week's edition. If you would like to contact customer service, they would be more than happy to assist you

with your reading plans. Thanks for reading with us and have a great
day.

How many times has this happened to you in the airline world?
When you finally find the customer service desk, it has a mile-long line
of weary travelers waiting to tell their woes to the stressed out agent.
What then? Do you wait in agony while watching your potential new
flights depart in front of you?

I have some better options for you.

1. **Reach out and touch someone.** Pick up the nearest phone and
   call the airline's customer service and reservation center. They can
   assist you with your itinerary and rebook you on the next available flight. If it requires a new ticket, tell them you will pick it up
   at the electronic check-in kiosk. The phone may be busy at first,
   but keep trying. Anything is better than waiting behind the people camping out in the other line. Ask if your airline has an electronic customer service kiosk. If they do, then you can revamp
   your itinerary and get a ticket there also. OK, you may be talking
   to an outsourced worker in Bangladesh, but when it comes to getting to your destination, morality takes an economy seat.

2. **It pays to carry a timetable of your airline's schedule.** Look up
   your connection possibilities from a different major city. It would
   be best if it was from one of your airline's major hub cities. Many
   times the agents can rebook you even if you are scheduled for a
   different flight.

3. **Be a frequent flier program member.** Many airlines give their
   elite members a special rebooking phone number in cases of cancellations. Ask for it and be adamant. I did a Google search and
   found the number for my airline. Also, go to your airline's member lounge and get assistance from the agent in there.

4. **Be alert.** If you are in the boarding area and you see the crew
   deplaning, it's time to take action, because that isn't a good sign.
   Also, if you hear the announcement or statement that the flight is
   on a "decision," start deciding on alternate travel plans. The word
   "decision" usually means trouble.

5. **Patience is a virtue.** Grab a magazine and a cup of coffee, and try to understand. There is a reason that the plane can't go to your destination just yet, and that reason is because it is not completely safe for travel. It's when they go despite mechanical problems that you have to start wondering about the airline you're flying with.

When you do experience this sort of delay or cancellation, remember this: the airline is responsible for payment and expenses due to your inconvenience. They have a contract with you to get you from point A to point B on the specified date and time. If anything (except weather) goes wrong once you get to point A, then they have not fulfilled their side of the deal and must rectify it.

Some airlines handle it well, while others are laughable. My last canceled flight was handled professionally. While the wait was occurring, passengers were given a $10 voucher for any of the facilities in the airport. When the cancellation notice was posted, my airline put the passengers up at a very nice hotel with dinner, a new flight time arranged for the next morning, and provided a free 15-minute long-distance phone call.

It may not seem like much, but with 300 people, it adds up. I have heard of stories of what other airlines had to offer, and it wasn't comparable. One airline recently got into trouble because they had passengers waiting for 34 hours at the gate without being given so much as a meal voucher.

The weather factor is another matter. Airlines have deemed it necessary not to pay for extras when it comes to weather. They say it would be the end of them if they did. So anything related to weather is not covered. It may be sunny and 75 degrees at your location, but if your airplane or crew does not show because of a snowstorm in North Dakota, then it becomes a weather situation. Airlines are quite the politicians when it comes to weatherable offenses.

All airlines encounter mechanical problems. At the end of the day, if you miss a connecting flight or a business meeting, fail to meet up with a loved one, or start the holiday off a little bit late, remember the most important thing. Your safety has not been compromised, and you will live another day. Others have not been as lucky.

CHAPTER SEVEN

Canceled Flight? Be the First to Know

I t pays to know when a cancellation is coming: Things to look out for:

"Your flight has been canceled." It happens to everyone sooner or later.

What you do next is important. Two minutes spent cursing the gods could mean the difference between getting home a few hours late and hitchhiking cross-country on standby. So it pays to know when a cancellation is coming.

Here are 10 early-warning signs that your flight may be canceled or seriously delayed. They all require you to use your powers of observation. Let's start with things to look out for before you board the plane.

1. **Shocking volume.** You see lightning and hear the thunder. If you can hear the rattle through the airport windows, you know the storm is too close for takeoff. Your flight may not be canceled, but you should prepare for a lengthy delay. Congestion can back up the airport for hours.

2. **Decisions, decisions.** The gate agent makes an announcement that the flight is on a "decision," and that you will get new departure information shortly. "Decision" means that Operation Control is determining if the airplane can go or not. It also means you should start deciding on a backup plan.

3. **Not even going to try.** The gate agent takes down the departure time from the marquee at the gate and leaves it blank. If they aren't even going to estimate the new departure time, you know it's going to be long wait.

4. **Let's all have lunch.** Meal vouchers are distributed for airport dining. The good airlines still do this as a matter of course, and it may mean nothing more than a short wait. But, considering the financial difficulty the industry is going through, when the lower-budget airlines decide to feed you, you know the situation is serious.

5. **De-plane truth.** You're at the gate waiting for the boarding announcement and you see your flight crew (pilots or flight attendants) start deplaning. This is almost a sure sign of impending cancellation. Why? Because the airline notifies the crew first so they can report to Crew Scheduling for possible reassignment.

Departure problems can also arise after you have boarded the plane. You're stuck now, but you can still use your cell phone to change plans if the situation starts to look really dicey. Here are five more things to look for.

1. **Like cops at a donut shop.** A group of mechanics comes on-board, and the flight attendants serve them all coffee. This usually means a big problem and you should not expect a quick departure.

2. **Distractions, distractions.** The flight attendants start the movie when you are still at the gate. It's a nice gesture and will take your mind off upcoming missed connections, but you should probably skip the show and use your time to call customer service to discuss other options.

3. **Heeding the call.** You are taxiing and the flight attendant gets a call from the cockpit. Look for an expression of frustration or disappointment. Usually what will follow is an announcement from the captain that you are returning to the gate. This usually means a serious problem has arisen.

4. **Kvetching in the back.** You have to arrange to intercept this early-warning sign. Next time you are delayed at the gate and the seat belt sign is off, get up and walk to the back galley. Now listen. If flight attendants are talking about their contract obligations and how this flight is going to ruin their days off, you're in trouble. But if they are talking about their layover plans, there is still hope for a takeoff.

5. **Duck, duck, goose.** The First Class concierge comes on-board and takes a few VIP passengers off with their bags. This usually means they are taking them to a different flight that will get them to their destination a lot faster. This may seem unfair, but VIPs are the airline's bread and butter. You'll have to fend for yourself, but you should think about doing the same.

Cancellations are a fact of life in the airline industry. Throwing a temper tantrum will only increase the time it takes to get where you're going. Don't join the crowd staring at the departure board in disbelief. Instead, be a smart traveler. Pay attention, have a backup plan, and keep your cell phone handy. With a little luck, you'll be on your way in no time.

10 Ways to Get an Upgrade

Y ou see them crowding the airport check-in counter, looking for a sign. Waiting for an announcement.

They are business travelers, frequent fliers, off-duty employees, and even first-timers. They are the last ones to board, but the first ones to petition for an available seat up front.

Every flight has its share of upgrade candidates. But there are usually more candidates than First Class seats, and as a result, some of those passengers become very upset. (If you're one of those people, here's a little something to ponder: If the airlines upgraded everyone, how would they make any money?)

Still, the upgrade brigade persists, even after the last person has boarded.

Among the arguments I've heard for reassigning a passenger to a premium seat: "My reading light doesn't work, my seat doesn't recline, I smell smoke, I have asthma, diarrhea, epilepsy, a heart condition. I am too tall, fat, old. I lost my boarding card, and the ground agent said I could take a seat anywhere. I hate this airline, love this airline, I work for another airline, I am an employee for this airline. My sister's ex-boyfriend's doctor's cousin's daughter used to fly for this airline."

They never work. Well, almost never.

One time a passenger had a heart attack, and we had a fairly empty First Class section. We moved him up there until we landed. But that's a pretty tough way to get more legroom.

I have had passengers shake my hand upon boarding and slip me twenties, fifties, and even hundred dollar bills asking me to "see what I can do for them." I even had a lady promise to induct me into the Mile High Club if I got her a higher-class seat.

It's not that the flight attendants don't want to upgrade you, it's just plain and simple: we can't. Our rules of conduct state specifically that upgrading (without permission from a supervisor on the ground or, in emergencies, from the captain) is an offense punishable by immediate discharge.

It's a firm rule, with no room for negotiation or interpretation.

Keep this in mind: you could have an airline employee eating right out of your hand, but when the magic word or implication of an upgrade arises, an alarm bell goes off in his head which discredits everything you have said up to that point. You've been made. We call it our BS alert.

But it can happen; here are some factors that will increase your chances of getting an upgrade:

1. Become a member of that specific airline's frequent flier mileage club. You can be a member of many different airline clubs.

2. The flight is oversold in Economy, but there are empty seats in Business and or First Class.

3. You are dressed smartly or in business attire. Jacket and tie for men and a dress/suit for women.

4. You are traveling alone. Sorry, if you're with kids, it's almost an automatic disqualifier.

5. Always be willing to move when asked. I know of a man who refused to move because he was seated on the aisle. What he didn't realize was that the seat they were offering him was in First Class.

6. Courtesy and kindness does go a long way in this industry—I have seen many people upgraded just because of the kindness they showed. I know when I am aboard, if someone is especially nice, I want to do something extra for him or her, and I'm positive the ground staff feel the same way.

7. Be early. Your chances of sitting up front diminish quickly when you inquire at the last minute.

8. If you have been seriously inconvenienced on a previous flight, make sure the check-in agents know about it. But don't make a scene or they will put you in the worst possible seat, hoping never to see you again.

9. Use the right card. Many times the credit card you pay with has a redeemable mile feature usable with several different airlines.

10. When you book the ticket, ask about upgrades and prices. There is a fare called Y-UP that costs a little more but increases your upgrade chances immensely. Many times there are ongoing promotions to spur First Class revenue. I paid full fare on an airline and was amazed when an extra $20 got me sitting in 1A. I can easily justify that cost in red wine.

Let's face it, domestic First Class, if there even is one, is probably not worth the upgrade effort, but I believe internationally, it is. It's not just about free drinks and slightly bigger seats; I am talking about gourmet food, premium wines, and seats that convert into beds. So if you strive for an upgrade, do it on an international flight.

If you find yourself up front on a future flight, have a glass of red wine for me. I recommend the California Cabernet my airline carries. Who knows, I might be the one pouring it for you.

Pass Your TSA Screening: 10 Tips

T SA doesn't stand for Thousands Standing Around, although sometimes it seems like it should.

Not only are there swarms of TSA employees everywhere, but
when you get to a line during rush hour, you too become one of the
thousands standing around. Nobody likes waiting around after being
told to take off some of your clothes, or watching as other passengers
ahead of you take an agonizingly long time being searched.

When you finally make it to the magnetometer, you are either annoyed or thoroughly disgusted.

TSA is run by the government and while many of you sneer at that
fact, try to remember how it was. I cringe every time I recollect the inefficient security of the old days. For me, the worst part was that most
of the personnel spoke little or no English.

When TSA took over, the joke among airline crewmembers was that TSA stood for "They Seem American."

Some say that airport security isn't any better than before 9/11; I strongly disagree. Air travel is safer now than it has ever been. I used to be appalled that airline employees were never screened. Now, nearly everyone is. It used to scare me that bags would go on a domestic flight regardless of whether the owner was on the plane (a process called baggage-matching). Airlines now have a 100-percent bag match rule, which, although it may cause a few delays, is being strictly enforced.

I used to think up ways of getting items past security. Those ways are now mostly gone.

Every day brings new security measures, from closer shoe inspection to high-tech machines. America and its airline industry cannot afford to have a repeat terrorist incident. So everything possible is being done to prevent such events.

Having said all of that, there are still some hassles along the way.

First and foremost, the lines at security are probably enough to turn you right off from air travel. In my case, I know that the shortest distance between two points is not the line that I seem to choose. Just as I get close to the front, something gets clogged up, while all the other lines are moving. Then, as I switch lines, the new one gets jammed and the one I left starts moving. I believe there are certain tricks of the trade that can get you through a bit more quickly and comfortably.

Here are 10 tips to help you through the new airport security procedures:

1. Put any sharp objects or any electrical devices you don't need on the flight into your checked luggage. As checked luggage is not accessible during the flight, such items are permitted in your bags.

2. Remove anything from your person that is remotely metallic, such as jewelry, watches, coins, etc., and put them in your carry-on bag that goes through the x-ray machine. This way, you won't set off the metal detector or risk forgetting items you put in the plastic tray.

3. Pick a line and stick to it. Bring a book—better yet, bring my book—to pass the time.

4. Walk through the metal detector in one brisk stride. Stopping halfway, or walking through slowly, often causes false alarms. If the alarm goes off on your first time through, you only get one more try before the full search, so double-check everything in your pockets and on your person.

5. If you are a frequent traveler and keep setting off the metal detector, listen and pay attention as the screener wands you. If your buttons trigger the alarm, next time wear different attire. Ladies, try to avoid bras with underwire support. The next time you fly you will know what to avoid wearing.

6. Watch your carry-on items when you are being waved with the security wand. Even with the added officials and video surveillance technology, opportunities for theft abound.

7. Don't cause a scene. I know it's frustrating to be singled out, but that tantrum you are about to throw could delay your journey over 30 minutes. You will be sent through every level of security checks they have, just on principle.

8. Please don't get mad at the airline crews when we go to the front of the line. How would you like to discover the reason for your flight delay was that the crew was held up at security?

9. Put on your MP3 player with your favorite music and watch with amusement the show taking place before you. People are naturally amusing, and the music adds a special touch to this comedy of life. It's like an ad-lib performance of synchronized swimmers. Of course, everyone will look at you oddly as you laugh, but who cares?

10. Speak up! I have said it before and I will say it again: If you witness a breach of security, tell someone immediately. Apparently, one day in August prior to the tragedy, a well-known actor had witnessed a breach of security involving a man at Boston's Logan Airport. He spoke up, but nothing was done. Later, authorities determined that the man was one of the 9/11 hijackers doing a practice run. They will listen to you now, I guarantee it. The life you save may be yours, but it may be mine as well.

Who knows what the future in security technology will bring? Full body x-rays, fingerprint scanners, and goggles where screeners can see through clothing are just a few items that are in the works. I read a security update that stated "rectal scanners" were being considered for major airports. I nearly choked until I realized that it was a typo intended to read "retinal scanners."

Even though it was a typo, it created a mind-blowing, malodorous image.

CHAPTER TEN

Top 10 Holiday Airport Sightings

I have been flying for more than 18 years. Some holidays I have been required to work and on others I have volunteered because of the extra pay involved. I remember when I began with Pan Am I would always work on my birthday, because I didn't want to be alone and maybe a female crewmember would give me some extra attention for a present. Hey, I was single and human, and it worked . . . usually.

Over the years, I have experienced or heard about some wild airport happenings around holidays, and I have always made it a point to write them down. Here is my list of the top 10 bizarre holiday airport sightings:

1. Santa was in full costume from his red satin pants to his flowing white beard, but he had a problem getting by security. He kept

setting off the metal detector, and some of the presents in his sack had to be opened. He was detained so long that he missed his flight. Where was he going? No, not the North Pole but North Dakota, close enough and cold enough, I guess. But where were the reindeer?

2. On Thanksgiving, a man and his pet turkey caused quite a commotion at Boston's Logan Airport when the bird flew the coop and escaped. I wasn't there, but can you imagine airport personnel, police officers, and an airport full of passengers engaged in a mass turkey hunt?

3. A man was much delayed at Chicago's O'Hare Airport (shocking, I know) one New Year's Eve. He was on his way to a fancy celebration party with two cases of chilled Dom Perignon Champagne. When midnight approached, he got some glasses from the terminal restaurant, opened every bottle, and enjoyed a very generous and expensive countdown toast with everyone within reach at the airport.

4. On July 4, a man was arrested for streaking through a Washington airport dressed only in an Uncle Sam hat and beard; an American flag extended from his—for lack of a publishable word—flagpole. I can't decide whether this act was stupid, disrespectful, funny, or all of the above. Regardless, I hear his flag was at half-mast when they took him away.

5. One Easter Sunday at LAX, a couple was arrested for entering a secure area and performing lewd and lascivious acts upon one another. Was it that they were dressed as rabbits or did the Hollywood influence take over?

6. Each year, U.S. customs officials confiscate hundreds of trees and plants; Arbor Day is an especially busy day for them. I flew in from London with a fellow flight attendant who got caught smuggling in a live rose bush. She was given a hefty fine. When she tried to use the Arbor Day excuse, the customs official pointed out that she had a bush, not a tree. She got cute and responded, "A rose by any other name is still a rose," whereupon the official increased the fine.

7. Now, it wouldn't be a true Labor Day unless a passenger went into labor on one of my flights. I was the purser when a lady went into premature labor. We called for a doctor who, fortunately, was able to stop the labor and give the baby some more time to develop. A month later, I received a photo of the baby and a card expressing gratitude. They didn't name the baby after me because it was a girl—or so I would like to think. One small note: I, too, was born on Labor Day, though not on an airplane.

8. One Christmas, I was waiting at the gate for an incoming airplane when a little boy dashed by clutching a Santa hat, wig, and beard. His happy squeals trailed behind him as he ran down the terminal and out of sight. Two minutes later, a scalped Santa galloped by, out of breath, searching for his top. He looked like a convertible caught in a rainstorm. The event brought cheer to everyone at the gate.

9. Crewmembers are permitted to dress in costume on Halloween flights. Most don't participate, but some wear mild outfits, and a select few do go to extremes. I have seen clowns, devils, Disney characters, pilots dressed as flight attendants and vice versa. One flight attendant went too far when he changed into his costume in the airplane restroom and emerged as a terrorist. He was detained by security and was fired soon afterward. I guess you could say that his Osama bin Laden costume bombed. I find it incredible that he actually thought people would be amused.

10. My favorite holiday sighting happened when I volunteered for the airline's traditional fantasy trip, which stages a Christmas flight to the North Pole for seriously ill children. The kids boarded the airplane, taxied around the airport and arrived at a hangar decorated as Santa's Village. To see the wonder and excitement in the children's eyes and to help them forget—however briefly—their daily round of sickness was priceless. I cried silently the entire time.

We take a lot for granted in this life. Try not to. This holiday season, breathe deeply, love freely, and laugh as much as you possibly can— simply because you can.

CHAPTER ELEVEN

Flying This Holiday? 10 Tips

T he holiday season is the time of year when airplanes are full, over-head bins are crammed tight, and the weather plays winter-delay games. At the airport, emotions run high and patience runs low, so get ready for a turbulent ride. Yes, holiday travel is stressful, but it needn't be beastly. Here are 10 tips to get you where you're going with your holiday cheer intact.

1. **Skip the cheap deal.** Many airlines offer big bargains for flights on Thanksgiving Day. You might save a bundle, but there is little worse than spending Thanksgiving at the airport with a bunch of airline employees and other passengers who don't want to be there. You think the holidays can be depressing? Just wait until your Thanksgiving feast consists of a turkey burrito. I speak from experience.

2. **Do a good deed.** Help the elderly lady with her luggage. Thank a passing soldier for his or her service to our country. Lend a hand with that baby. It's proven that the more good deeds you do for others, the better it makes you feel.

3. **Don't weather the storm.** Avoid connecting through airports with known weather problems. For example, if you are flying from Los Angeles to Florida, don't connect through Chicago or New York. Pay the extra money and go nonstop if possible. Believe me, the less chance for tie-ups, the better.

4. **Adjust your attitude.** Holiday travel is a mind game. If you expect your flight to be a nonstop pain in the neck, then it probably will be. If you approach it as an adventure with interesting ups and downs, you might actually enjoy yourself. Personally, I love holiday flying because it brings out the variety in passengers, and there is always a sense of excitement in the air.

5. **Wrap later.** Don't wrap your presents before you leave. If you do, security agents might be opening your gifts instead of your loved ones, and you'll be wrapping them all over again. Also, removing the batteries from toys and electronic items will save you many hassles at check-in and security.

6. **Pack it in.** Holiday presents mean lots of big bundles and, no, they won't all fit in the overhead bin. Be sensible and check some of it in. Also be sure to pack an empty bag inside your luggage, as you will undoubtedly have lots of big presents to cope with on the return flight.

7. **Don't fly off the handle.** Your flight cancels, the airport shuts down, you miss your connection, your flight is overbooked, your luggage disappears—the chances of holiday misadventure are high. How you react will set the tone for your whole holiday. I once had a passenger get so mad that he had a stroke and spent Christmas in intensive care. So, stop! Count to 10, put yourself in someone else's shoes, laugh, have a drink—do whatever it takes to avoid an outburst or a scene.

8. **Feel secure.** It is very easy to ridicule the Transportation Security Administration. I know, because I do it all the time. Its agents poke into your bags, create long lines, enforce silly rules, are often inconsistent, but they are responsible for keeping your flight safe. They are doing their jobs as they have been trained to do, and they have to deal with thousands of upset passengers every day. Do you remember what passed for security before 9/11? I do and, believe me, I am very thankful for the new system.

9. **Be politically incorrect.** I am so tired of generic holiday greetings. Say "Merry Christmas," "Happy Hanukah," "Habari Gani," or whatever you believe in. Just say something heartfelt. And while you're at it, wear a Santa hat or other festive attire. You will brighten the atmosphere instead of adding to the gloom in the gate area.

10. **Just do it.** Don't put off traveling just because of the hassles involved. If you have someone to enjoy the holidays with, just do it. Last Thanksgiving, my favorite uncle invited me to a big turkey dinner but I declined, not wanting to deal with flying standby on the holidays. I took the extra holiday pay instead. My uncle passed away a few months ago, and now I would pay anything to have made it to that dinner.

I am often delayed at certain airports when I am working the holiday season. My favorite pastime in this situation is to bring out my portable music player. I cue my Christmas playlist of favorite holiday songs, then sit back and watch all the holiday travelers. Airports are full of strange and wonderful people and, with a little festive music playing in the background, it's like watching a reality-show version of *The Nutcracker.*

May your delays be minimal, your flights be safe, and your holiday season full of cheer. Don't ever forget why you are enduring the hassles of holiday air travel. It's because someone on the other end is eagerly anticipating your arrival.

CHAPTER TWELVE

Call Me Cranky: 10 Rules for Your Cell

Ah, cell phones—the gadgets that are so dear to our hearts, pockets, and purses. I don't know how we ever survived air travel without them. It's so easy now to keep in touch with our loved ones and colleagues—to inflict on them all our boredom as we sit at the gate, all our worry about tight connections, even that sudden panic about the coffeepot back home (did I turn it off?).

People used to strike up conversations with real people at the airport. Now they walk around with one hand glued to the side of their heads talking into little microphones, saying things like "Yeah, the airplane's pretty big" and "Did Lulu get her breakfast?"

But cell phones are here to stay. So, in the humble manner that befits my station as a flight attendant, I offer 10 tips for cell-phone use in and around the airport.

1. **Call later.** Fact: Cell-phone use has not been proven to interfere with sensitive instruments in the cockpit—at least not in any way that would cause a major disruption. Nevertheless, there are times when it is a bad idea to use a cell phone and others when it is outright forbidden. For example, you cannot use a cell phone when going through customs, during the safety demo, or at any time in-flight. Not that my phone works mid-flight anyway, but I am sure there are phones that do by now.

2. **Check your ring tones.** Everyone has his own way of being alerted to an incoming call—be it funny, annoying, loud, or silently vibratory. Just two rules here. First, be courteous to your fellow travelers by keeping your phone nearby and turned to low (or vibrate). Second, don't be an idiot. A man at O'Hare Airport was arrested for having a ring tone of someone screaming "Bomb!" followed by the sounds of an explosion and laughter in the background. He pleaded stupidity and got off easily, only missing his flight.

3. **Censor yourself.** I don't know about you, but I find myself tuning in to the conversations taking place in cramped public places. So if your cell-phone conversation includes personal information, try not to broadcast it to the world. I was once in a crowded gate area when a cell caller described in detail his recent colonic irrigation. Way too much information.

4. **Beware the automated operator.** More and more often these days, customer-service operators turn out to be computers. Inquire about a flight to Boston, and you may get information on a flight to Narita instead. Dealing with tone-deaf computers can turn your good mood sour. My wife is the sweetest woman, but put her on the phone with a computer that can't handle her English accent, and you have a fire-breathing dragon on your hands. If you find yourself in a similar situation, head to a corner because the yelling could be quite jarring to innocent bystanders. Computer: "I think you said Narita." Wife: "Boston, you stupid f-ing computer, Boston!!!!"

5. **Don't be ear-itating.** If you have one of those streamlined earpieces, realize that people may think you are talking to yourself—or to

them. It's my job to answer questions at the airport, and I'm forever getting snippy responses of "No, not you!" from folks whose earpieces I never saw. I think these people should have a neon placard on their foreheads saying, "No, I'm not crazy, I'm on the phone."

6. **Degadgetize.** There is not a cell phone in existence that can go through security without setting off the metal detector. So if you usually clip yours to an inside pocket, holster it on your side, or keep it tucked away in some nether region of your clothing, do yourself (and the many people in line behind you) a favor and set it free when you first get in line.

7. **Call before you board.** Maybe the reason they don't want you using your cell phone in-flight is to make you use the pay phone on the airplane instead. Holy cow, have you taken a look at the prices? They are around $10 for the connection fee and $10 a minute! The way airfares are these days, that phone call could cost you more than the actual flight.

8. **Center of the universe.** If you are one of those people who can't walk and talk at the same time, then get out of the way. There are probably hundreds of people behind you trying to get to a gate or to the baggage claim. Just head for a pay phone and chat on your cell phone from there. No one is using those pay phones anyway.

9. **Call-waiting areas.** Realize that many airports have areas for people to wait in their cars until you have landed and are ready to be picked up. This prevents the grumpy airport traffic cop from yelling at them as they crawl along at one mile per hour in the Arrivals lane trying to look inconspicuous. So do make a call after you touch down, but try to save the long version of your trip for the ride home.

10. **Don't leave home without it.** Even if you're going to a place where your phone won't work, or you don't want to be contacted, bring your cell phone along anyway. It probably has an alarm clock that could come in handy, or a game that can pass the time. And remember, when you don't want to talk to someone anymore, you can always hang up and blame it on the connection.

Cell phones have changed air travel a lot, even in the airplane cabin, where they have dramatically cut down on the goodbyes at the end of a flight. Now approximately eight out of every 10 passengers exiting the plane are engrossed in very important conversations and merely nod goodbye to me. Luckily, I don't get paid per "Buh-Bye."

News flash: Legislation is now in the works to allow cell-phone use in-flight. Can you imagine 300 people in a metal tube rambling on and on? Do you think this is a good idea or a bad idea? You can text message me from your phone on . . . No, just joking.

CHAPTER THIRTEEN

10 Tips for Getting Through Customs

How many times have you returned from your international trip and the first people you encounter are the smiling group at Customs and Immigration, greeting you with open arms? Okay, more likely you encounter somewhat grumpy personnel with extended palms, wanting your passport or customs declaration.

Who are these men and women who ask you personal questions about your recent trip, have full permission to look through your bags and search your person? Well, they aren't employed by the airlines or airport, but by the federal government. So they don't have to be nice and will always have a pension.

If the customs officials weren't doing this job, I wonder what they would be doing. Let's just say that I don't think they would be greeters at Wal-Mart. They're not there to be social directors, and very rarely do I see them happy. Maybe it's because they see thousands of people a day, and in the seconds of interaction with each passenger, they have to decide if a person is entering the country illegally, or bringing in something they shouldn't.

First stage is Immigration and Passport Control, followed by Customs, where you find Agricultural Inspection and, if necessary, secondary screening. If anything illegal is found at the secondary stage, get ready for the personal searches and, yep, the rubber gloves. I have been strip searched by customs in Thailand and, believe me, it happens here as well.

Have you ever seen a customs official walking a small dog through the baggage area? No, it's not for the exercise. That dog is there looking, or I should say smelling, for any forbidden fruits or produce. I know this for a fact because it caught me with an apple in my bag. It got all excited when it got to my suitcase. So, in the end, he got his Scooby snack and it cost me $100. I hear that I got off lightly.

Here are some of my tips for getting through Customs and Immigration a bit easier:

1. If you know you will have a tight connection when you land in the U.S., leave the flowers or produce behind. Agriculture inspection sometimes adds up to one hour or more.

2. Always carry a photocopy of your passport separately from your passport. Many officials will accept it if you misplace it.

3. Turn your cell phones off. Customs and Immigration are strict on that rule and will confiscate and not return them.

4. Don't make wisecracks or jokes to the officials; it only makes you look like you are trying to hide something.

5. Read your forms carefully, and fill them out as soon as you get them. There is a complete guide to filling out your form and a list of contraband items at the back of your in-flight magazine.

6. If you are unsure, declare it. The "I didn't know reply" won't work.

7. Don't make a scene. If it's a long wait and your connecting flight is soon, so is everyone else's and you definitely won't make your flight if you are sent to secondary screening.

8. If you are uncomfortable with the opposite sex searching through your luggage, ask for an official of the same sex. Many travelers don't know that they can make such a request.

9. Don't put any fruit in your bag during your vacation. You may have carried around some mangos in a sack a week ago but the persistent aroma will have the fruit dog all over it and you will be delayed in agriculture.

10. Leave any photos or videos of you and a partner in a compromising position at home. They could be considered pornography, and when they are confiscated, they will probably go up on their "wall of shame" in some back office.

These officials must have enough stories to fill a book. During my own years as a flight attendant, I witnessed the following incidents and items being seized: a full grown hidden rose bush, extensive sex toy collection, an Indian lady with 18 suitcases, a satanic knife collection, a middle-aged Asian man with 24 bottles of cognac, a young man with a leg flask containing bourbon that broke and created a "pissed-in-his-pants" effect, an Iranian woman with stacks of cash equaling $210,000, a passenger with 300 fake Rolex watches, and a man dressed in solid yellow attire with a collection of inflatable female dolls (we named him the Banana Harem).

Passengers aren't the only ones to get caught red-handed trying to bring something through. Crewmembers have been apprehended smuggling everything from computer chips to fake Gucci bags. But no story equals that of the infamous "Monkey Stew." He was a flight attendant who worked a regular route from the U.S. to South America. He'd discovered that a certain species of baby monkey that cost $500 in Brazil would fetch up to $10,000 in the states. He developed a system where he would drug an animal with a 12-hour sedative, bribe an agent to get his bag past security, deliver his package to a person on the other side, and collect quite a mark-up each trip. It was considered animal smuggling and highly illegal, but with four trips a month, he was raking it in.

One day his intended destination was closed due to fog. With the delay, the flight was close to 12 hours long. The sedated monkey, hopefully, would remain sleeping. He made it past Immigration, but started to feel a rustling coming from his specially designed monkey carrier. He started to panic and began sweating profusely.

Almost in the clear, the monkey gave out an initial yell and the flight attendant started to walk faster. The monkey was waking up and was making muffled screeches every two strides. He approached the oldest customs agent, hoping he was hard of hearing. As the flight attendant was cleared through the final stage, the monkey screamed at the top of his lungs.

Apparently, it was the funniest sight, a grown man in uniform in the prone position, five customs officials surrounding him, and a baby monkey sitting on top of the carrier sounding as if it were laughing at the man. The flight attendant lost his job, was sent to jail as an animal smuggler, and had his picture in the newspapers, branded with the nickname of "Monkey Stew."

Monkey Stew is now out of jail and paying his fine by working in an exotic pet store. The story is a well known and documented case. It wasn't the first case of animal smuggling and I am sure it won't be the last, because as you all know, "Monkey see, monkey do!"

PART TWO

In the Air

CHAPTER ONE

How to Fly Happy

We all know that in-flight, as in life, people have their good moments and their bad moments. Nobody is happy all the time just as no one is always in a foul mood (although I have met a few candidates for the latter distinction). When we're stuck in a metal tube eight miles in the air with no food to serve, I try to engage the happy travelers in an attempt to learn their secret.

I've asked, and I've heard an earful. The following is a list of responses from happy travelers that I have encountered in-flight.

1. **Don't let one mishap ruin your whole trip.** If you run into a rude flight attendant or are delayed and miss your connection, try to put it behind you. After all, you have the whole rest of your trip ahead of you. Just shrug "So what?" and move on.

2. **Get there early.** Leave enough time for the inevitable hassles: traffic jams on the way to the airport, check-in snafus, bathroom breaks for toddlers, slow-moving lines at security—you name it. I have met very few stressed-out passengers who are happy.

3. **Be kind to your fellow travelers.** Not for them but for you. Courtesy and kindness are contagious and soul-satisfying. And, no, there's nothing wrong with doing something unselfish for selfish reasons.

4. **Don't brood about what might have been.** If you can't get the upgrade, the special seat, or the rerouting you were hoping for, let it go. Equanimity makes for a more pleasant flight.

5. **Listen to music you like.** Your iPod makes you a happier traveler. Why? Because when you listen to music you want to hear, the world seems like a better place. Your MP3 player can even make frustrating situations tolerable. Next time you're stuck in a flight delay, crank up the music and let your fellow travelers star in your own private "reality music video."

6. **Bring a happy place.** Carry a small photo collection with you, where you can go to focus on what really matters in life. Now that MP3 players have digital photo players on them, you can upload your favorite memories and listen to music at the same time.

7. **Keep busy.** Bring a Sudoku collection, a computer, a DVD player, a good book, homework, a book of riddles, letters to read, or anything else to keep your mind off the usual worries and annoyances. As the saying goes, "Busy is much better than bored."

8. **Be open-minded.** When you fly, you encounter many different people with many different beliefs, styles, looks and—yes—even smells. Open your mind to a new world of possibilities. Even if you don't agree with someone's choices, accept and embrace the differences that exist in all of us.

9. **See the glass half full, not half empty.** It's not what happens, but how you think about what happens. If your plane has a mechanical problem that causes a delay or cancellation, you could go into a tirade about your bad luck or you could be thankful that noth-

ing will go wrong midflight. There is a good side to everything in life; you just have to find it.

10. **Laugh it up.** I believe the most important asset in travel, and in life, is the ability to laugh at yourself. If you can't laugh at yourself, you can't really have fun. My wife and I have been married for 14 years now, and we spend most of our time together laughing. If we've survived that long on laughter, surely you can laugh your way through a flight from Atlanta to Denver.

On one of my flights, I had an older gentleman as a passenger who beamed with smiles and had spells of all-out laughter. He kept this up the whole flight, even though the plane was full, service was slow and he was crammed into a middle seat. At times he laughed so hard, tears would trickle down his cheeks. When I asked what was so funny, he said he'd let me know at the end of the flight.

When we landed and most of the passengers had disembarked, the gentleman pulled me aside and told me he had a remote-control fart-noise machine in his carry-on bag; it was a gift for his grandson. He had put it in an overhead bin away from his own seat, near an obnoxious passenger who was complaining about everything. Every time the complainer started to whine, the older man would push a button and a different unmentionable sound would erupt over the malcontent's head.

Apparently, the fart machine had the whole row in hysterics for most of the flight, until the loudmouth was finally silenced. The old gentleman said he had never laughed so hard in his life, and that his grandson was going to have to wait for his gift because he was keeping this one for himself.

Okay, remote-control devices are no longer allowed on-board U.S. aircraft, but it just goes to show that laughter can make a big difference.

So next time you fly, take some tips from the smiling side of the aisle. Don't worry. Be happy.

Stranded on the Runway

I n February, JetBlue made headlines by holding passengers hostage for over 10 hours on one of its planes in New York. A month later, a Royal Air Maroc flight from JFK to Casablanca held its passengers on-board for a record 16.5 hours before finally canceling the flight.

While these times are extraordinarily long, the practice of retaining passengers is an offense committed by most airlines at some time or another. These types of incidents happen every year, but nothing is ever really done about it. Sure, talk has resurfaced about a Passenger's Bill of Rights, but who would enforce it? And what can be done about the underlying problems that cause these nerve-racking runway waits?

Why does it happen at all?

1. Weather is the usual culprit. Snow, ice, lightning, strong winds, and hail all create havoc even for the most efficient airport operations. Most of the passenger-hostage situations are weather-related.

2. Traffic problems can create space shortages at airports. It's a domino situation: Incoming flights cannot pull up to their gates because they are occupied by other airplanes, so the incoming airplane must wait on the runway.

3. Delays can create unbelievably long lines for takeoff. In fact, I was once on a flight that was 165th for takeoff. But returning to the gate is almost always a no-no. Why? Because the flight will lose its place in the line.

4. Construction projects. Airports are always undergoing construction and renovation. Closing all runways except one at a busy airport like O'Hare or Hartsfield at rush hour will definitely make passengers feel that they count for nothing.

5. Alternate destinations. When your flight is diverted from your intended airport to another one, you will have plenty of other diverted aircraft for company. The new destination is often unaccustomed to handling a large volume of aircraft, and the mess just grows from there.

6. Aye, aye, Captain. Ultimately, it is all up to the captain. He or she has the final say about whether you return to the gate or not.

As a flight attendant, I have been snowed in at the Denver airport, stuck at Dallas-Fort Worth for days, and trapped on an O'Hare flight for six hours. I have also been on many flights where we held passengers for three hours or more against their will. So, in a sense, I have been both hostage and kidnapper.

There are two ways to look at the situation:

1. There should be an airline-wide maximum wait time for passengers already on-board an airplane. Airlines cannot keep treating passengers like cattle and expect complacency.

2. The goal of the airlines is to get passengers from point A to point B as quickly and as safely as possible. Any return-to-gate requirement by the government will have a negative effect on those passengers who are anxious to get to point B. Also, any compensation awarded to "hostage" passengers will be paid through price hikes that other passengers will pay for. My position is somewhere in the middle.

With the already-overpopulated skies becoming more crowded each year, and knowing full well that this problem will continue, I offer the following tips for dealing with runway hostage situations.

1. **Don't stop.** If you can pay a little bit more and fly to your destination nonstop, you should do so. Your chances of getting stuck on an airplane increase immensely with every intermediate connection.

2. **Keep informed.** Insist to a flight attendant that the pilots give 30-minute updates, and ask for a specific return time to the gate.

3. **Be firm but stay calm.** Feel free to express your concerns but don't get hostile. Hostility might get you back to the gate, but it could also land you in jail.

4. **Take your business elsewhere.** If you have suffered an extended runway delay more than once on one airline and have not received adequate explanation or compensation, change airlines. Yes, this happens to all airlines, but it seems to happen to some more than others.

5. **Get a temperature adjustment.** If you are suffering because of the cabin temperature, and the crew is unable to rectify the situation during a long hold, demand that the pilot either fix it or let you off the airplane. I have been on way too many flights where the humid heat of summer or the cold bite of winter has made the cabin environment unbearable.

6. **Try to sleep.** You could get all upset and let this ruin your trip, or you could sit back and try to get some shut-eye. Don't forget

to use your earplugs in case the pilot makes his every-30-minute rolling delay announcement.

7. **Bring back-up grub.** Many airlines carry very little food these days, so you find yourself not only stuck but starving, which only aggravates the situation. Bring a back-up bag of trail mix or a nutrition bar that can get you through the stomach growls.

8. **Alert the media.** If you are stuck on an airplane for more than four hours, call the news. The media love stories like these and the airlines hate this type of attention. In fact, I've often wondered why passengers held forever on the runway don't just call 911 and report a hostage situation. Is there any law against it?

9. **Drive instead.** If airport conditions look iffy, and your flight is less than an hour long, you might want to think about driving instead. Often, if you add up the time it takes you to get to the airport, go through security, fly the short route, and rent a car, you could already be there. You might want to think about this even if it looks like your flight will come and go on time. Just because you're traveling doesn't mean you have to fly.

10. **Demand money.** After such an ordeal, demand a cash payment, travel credit, mileage points, or other form of compensation from the airline to force the company to understand that you have been treated badly. Do this not only for yourself but also as a blow for passenger rights.

Good luck out there. I hope these tips help, and I'll see you on the runway.

CHAPTER THREE

12 Tips for a Better Flight

Want to have a better flight? Of course you do! And who better to give you some in-flight tips than a flight attendant whose favorite hobby is passenger-watching? I observe in amusement as travelers make the same mistakes, flight after flight.

So what makes the difference between a "horrible" and a "not so bad" trip? Here are 12 tips:

1. **Plug 'em up.** Earplugs are a wonderful invention, but seldom used. They can be bought for less than $1, and I can't stress their importance enough. Just think—no more crying babies, annoying seat chatter, or startling pilot announcements. The whole world seems a lot more tolerable when you use them. They work great in hotel rooms as well. I never leave home without them.

2. **Don't be part of a smelly situation.** A small tube of lavender lotion can be your saving grace when it comes to the in-flight body odors swirling around. A dab under your nostrils will leave you smiling while others gag at the nearby passenger with foot rot.

3. **Have some taste.** If you have the unusual experience of being fed onboard, skip the special meal unless it's a medical necessity. "Special meal" usually means a not-so-special taste.

4. **Bag it.** Don't check out your common sense with your check-in baggage. For example: heart medication, priceless heirlooms, passports, or items resembling weapons. Being reunited with your bags is not always an immediate guarantee. US Airways made this point abundantly clear during a recent holiday season.

5. **BYOA.** Bring your own amenities. Whether it's pillows, food, blankets, special requirements, magazines, antacid, or whatever, bring your own because airlines are slimming down on all amenities.

6. **Be a pessimistic optimist — or is it the other way around?** Don't expect every detail to go as planned. Delays, misconnects, and seat problems are just a few hassles associated with flying. It's unusual to make it through an entire journey without something going wrong.

7. **Cover thy laptop.** When any form of liquid passes near or over your personal solitaire machine, close the cover. I have witnessed accidents, turbulence, and clumsy flight attendants ruin too many computers in-flight.

8. **Chat her up.** Talk to your seat neighbors once in awhile. They could surprise you and be quite interesting. If not, you can say you tried and will probably never see them again. I have met some of the most interesting people in my life on an airplane. If you don't try, you'll never know.

9. **Carry on considerately.** It is time to be sensible if you are one of the growing number of frequent travelers who carry on their bags. A perfect-sized rollerboard suitcase is one that fits in the overhead bin wheels first and slides to the back. You are taking the space

of three other bags if you have to put it in sideways. Save the aggravation of finding a space and consider getting one that fits. I flew with the same passenger three times in the last month, and every time he told me it fit on his last flight, I assured him that I knew otherwise.

10. **Gadgetize yourself.** On your next flight bring an iPod, DVD player, or your kid's Gameboy to keep you distracted. I can't tell you how many times I have preserved what's left of my sanity by playing my $5 digital Yahtzee game.

11. **Check your mental baggage but carry on your sense of humor.** Air travel these days is stressful, nerve-racking and can be quite frustrating. If you look beyond these annoyances, you can often find interesting and quite humorous aspects.

12. **Give them a small break.** I know that airline employees can frustrate the hell out of you, but they are fighting for their lives and with less manpower and support. The workload of the gate agents, customer service reps, flight attendants, and even the pilots has recently doubled, but their pay has been halved. It takes a big person to be able to put the shoe on the other foot.

CHAPTER FOUR

Granny Isn't Exactly Sleeping

I have seen death on an airplane only a few times in my 17 years as a flight attendant, but I can remember each time as if it happened yesterday. I relive each occurrence over and over, wondering if there was anything anyone could or should have done differently.

My first experience was with a man who choked on a piece of meat. Instead of making a spectacle of himself, he went to the lavatory, where he was found an hour later—blue and quite dead. While the in-flight meal probably wasn't very good, I can't say it was to blame. No, the killer was humility, or perhaps pride. Surely, it is better to suffer an embarrassing scene and seek immediate help than to succumb in silence.

The second death occurred when an elderly man died in his sleep on a flight that was completely full. His wife, who realized what had happened, chose not to alert the passengers or flight crew so as not to make a scene. When the flight was over and all the other passengers had deplaned, she waved me over and told me that her husband had passed on. I thought she said "passed out," so I asked whether her husband was on any medications or if this had happened before. She replied that they were expecting his death for some time and that he had been dead for the final four hours of the flight.

The last incident was on a full flight home from Europe. I noticed a woman sitting next to a seat that held an urn neatly strapped in with a seat belt. The woman told me that her husband had passed away on vacation. Since the airline was not going to refund the money for her husband's ticket, and since she would prefer no one sit next to her, she had simply parked the ashes in the next seat. She was within her rights and seemed quite sensible about the whole situation. It was only later in the flight, when she decided to drink part of his ashes with hot water, that I thought she might have become a little unhinged.

It is true that the airlines will not refund any portion of a ticket that goes unused due to death, illness, or accident. In fact, the airline will charge you extra to transport the body home, as a casket requires special handling.

Here's another story—maybe true, maybe legend. Apparently a family from Mexico traveled to the United States for a family funeral. There were two young men, a girl, a mother, and a rather elderly grandmother in a wheelchair. The mother and daughter cried for most of the flight, while the young men attended to their grandmother. Then the daughter went to the back of the airplane for a drink, and began talking with a Spanish-speaking flight attendant. The attendant got quite a shock when the girl revealed the truth: "Granny isn't exactly sleeping." The family was indeed on the way to a funeral, but it was a funeral for their grandmother—the same one who came aboard in the wheelchair. Apparently, the family wasn't able to pay the extra charge for a casket to be carried in the cargo hold. While this particular story may be hard to believe, I am sure some variation of it has happened somewhere.

While the airlines don't give breaks when it comes to refunds or special handling, they do provide something called a "bereavement fare." If you have to purchase a last-minute ticket because of a death in the family, the airline won't gouge your savings account (as they often do when you buy a regular short-notice ticket).

Here are some things you need to know about bereavement fares:

1. Bereavement fares are for family members traveling to funerals or visiting a gravely ill family member. Proper documentation will be asked for and verified.

2. Eligible family members include spouse, children, parents, grand-parents, in-laws, step-parents, aunts and uncles, siblings, nieces and nephews; most airlines accept same-sex partners as well.

3. They aren't necessarily the lowest fares, but they are fares that can be purchased right up until the time of departure. Discounts range from 15 to 70 percent off full fare, and most often come in at 50 percent.

4. The fares are flexible, permitting free changes and stays up to 30 days (there is no minimum stay). If you have already purchased a ticket, the airline can change dates or allow deviations to original itineraries.

5. Bereavement fares are not available for all destinations, and international bereavement fares are rarely available. Still, you should always ask.

6. You will need the name of the person who is deceased or ill, as well as the name, address, and phone number of the health-care facility and doctor taking care of the patient. You will also need a copy of the death certificate (if applicable). If you cannot obtain a death certificate until after the funeral, a discount will be applied to the fare after presentation of the document.

7. Most airlines will allow you to use frequent flyer points, and they will waive any program restrictions provided there are flights available, but you should definitely double-check on this.

Death is never an easy topic, and when a family member dies, the last thing on your mind is ticket prices. Perhaps you will never be confronted with this situation, but odds have it that most of us will be. So keep these tips in mind. Someday they may make a difficult time a little bit easier.

CHAPTER FIVE

Air Travel: The Right Stuff

S ure, it's easy to get on the air-travel hate wagon, and I admit I enjoy poking fun at the airline industry sometimes myself. And why not? There is just so much to ridicule, and as a flight attendant, I constantly see the stupidity that the airlines try to ignore. But in this chapter I'd like to take a small break from what's wrong with air travel and take a quick look at the right stuff.

1. **Safety.** Despite terrorist threats and a huge increase in airplane traffic, air travel is safer now than ever. The National Transportation Safety Board and the Federal Aviation Administration now investigate each and every accident, and follow up with new safety procedures to reduce repeat occurrences. Yes, your flight might be delayed by a warning light or canceled because of a mechanical

problem, but your chances of making it to your destination in one piece have been improved dramatically.

2. **Choices.** With the increase in the number of airlines has come a wealth of new options. If one airline charges too much or treats you badly, you can almost always find a different carrier to get you where you are going. Remember the days when you often had to pay a fortune to an airline you couldn't stand? Well, thanks to Southwest Airlines and other low-cost carriers, you truly have a choice now.

3. **In-flight food.** Remember the lukewarm in-flight meal that was called "Salisbury Steak" but tasted like a salty piece of shoe? They said it was complimentary, but of course you paid for it in that sky-high ticket price. Now, on many flights, you have a choice whether to pay for it or not, plus the snacks on-board have gotten better. Of course, you have to pay for those, too.

4. **Airline alliances.** It is always a hassle when your flight is canceled or you miss your connecting flight, but new airline alliances improve your chances of making up lost time, as you can often take a convenient flight on a cooperating partner airline. Same goes for your mileage points: You can often use your frequent-flier miles to get a ticket on a partner airline to an exotic location.

5. **Fewer bumps.** While the skies produce the same turbulence as before, communication with air traffic control and between other flights has become much more prevalent. Shared information allows pilots and air traffic control to vector around trouble spots, making your flight much smoother. It also gives more adequate notice to the flight attendants, who can prepare the cabin when turbulence is unavoidable. I once got a call from the cockpit telling me to prepare for moderately choppy weather in 23 minutes. Not 22 minutes or 24 minutes, but 23. I decided to time it and it was indeed exactly 23 minutes.

6. **The Internet.** The World Wide Web is truly a wonderful thing. It's where we learn, work, communicate, and explore. It has even improved air travel. Not only can you find the best deals, you can

also check in, choose your seat, and check the status of your flight online—and read about the industry like you are doing now.

7. **Modern technology.** While I would like to see the Internet and wi-fi become available on more flights, you have to admit that many airlines have come a long way with personal video screens, multiple channels, video games, and even live television. Gone are the days of the tubular headset, bad audio, and bad screen quality—to say nothing of the same movie shown over and over again. And now if you're stuck with nine bad movies to choose from, you can play your own movie instead.

8. **Security.** Yes, the Transportation Security Administration. No matter how frustrating, inconsistent, and inefficient it may be, this agency has prevented any major terrorist incident from occurring. I, for one, feel a lot safer knowing the TSA is around. Remember the quality of security that was in place before 9/11? Now, *that* was scary.

9. **Smoke-out.** Air travel has improved dramatically since the ban on in-flight smoking was implemented over a decade ago. There are fewer fires, the cabin air is cleaner, and you smell a lot better at the end of a flight. I always thought it was ridiculous to say that Row 35 was in the "nonsmoking" section when folks in Row 36 were free to light up any time. Still, I think it's a bit overboard for airports to go totally smoke-free. I am not a smoker, but I do think airports could set aside one area outdoors for the die-hard puffers.

10. **Beats driving any day.** You never quite appreciate air travel until you are forced to drive for several days straight. After 9/11, when all U.S. airplanes were grounded, I had to drive from the East Coast to the West Coast. I would gladly take the smallest seat in economy and pay any price rather than endure that journey again.

CHAPTER SIX

Air Travel: The Wrong Stuff

O kay, so you've read about everything that is right with air travel. At the end of that piece, which was a Tripso.com column, I solicited readers' comments about what might be wrong with air travel. Now comes the fun part: your pet peeves.

Before I get started, I would like to make one point clear to the many people who will no doubt be wanting to write to me to complain about the following list. I did not write the responses, you did. If a complaint was made more than once, I put it on the list—whether it was serious, funny, trivial, or bizarre. My own comments are *in italics*. Without further ado, here it is: what's wrong with air travel.

In the Terminal

1. **Longer lines and fewer employees.** *This was the top complaint.*

2. **Customs and Immigration.** The lines and the inefficient procedures are a nightmare and getting worse.

3. **Wheelchair attendants.** How come these guys never meet the airplane on time and can't speak more than a few words of English? *I have to admit that, as a flight attendant, this is one of my pet peeves as well.*

4. **"Federal regulations require."** What exactly do federal regulations require? In the security area, especially, federal regulations seem to change from week to week and airport to airport. Other requirements vary widely from airline to airline, though the explanation is always "Federal regulations require . . ." Make an across-the-board policy and stick to it at every airport.

5. **Additional screening.** If my 80-year-old grandmother gets sent to secondary screening but Moammar Hussein does not, there is something very wrong.

6. **Arrival monitors inside the gate area.** Who cares about arriving flights when the only people permitted past security are ticketed passengers? *Good point. I never thought about that. I mean, there just aren't that many arriving passengers meeting other arriving passengers, although many clever passengers use the arrival monitors to see if the airlines are being honest about departure times and inbound airplanes.*

7. **Boarding procedures.** It's time to figure out how to board passengers in a more efficient manner. This is the 21st century.

On the Airplane

1. **Smaller seats and bigger people.** Do the airlines not know that most people are over 5'3" and 150 pounds?

2. **Old flight attendants with attitudes.** *Apparently, quite a few of*

you have recently traveled on international Pacific flights and have had the same crew of pissed-off grandmothers.

3. **Carry-on luggage.** *It was so nice after the London bomb scare when nobody was allowed any carry-on. Boarding was quicker and easier, and the flights went so much smoother.*

4. **In-flight lavatories.** By the end of the flight they are so disgusting that if you are forced to use one, you just want to cry—or pass out.

5. **Airlines that serve Pepsi instead of Coke.** Really? Of all the things wrong in the airline industry, you see soda pop as a major issue? *Apparently three of you did.*

6. **The seat-belt police.** "Come on!" complains one reader. "The seat-belt sign goes on, the cockpit makes an announcement, flight attendants check everybody's seat belt, and then, when somebody desperately has to use the facilities, they shout at the top of their lungs, "FASTEN YOUR SEAT BELTS!" We're not in elementary school anymore. If you gotta go, you gotta go. Would you rather I wet the seat?" *I sympathize, but here's another point of view: When you are out of your seat, you are endangering the people around you, who can get hurt if you get thrown around the cabin.*

7. **Germs and worse.** It never fails: When I go on a trip, I always catch something. They say the onboard air filters catch most of everything, but most is not all. Why do you think the man with tuberculosis was such a threat to his fellow passengers? Whether it be SARS, TB, or the next chemical concoctions of terrorists, people who fly are at risk. *All true—but you've got to be careful when you mix hypochondria with paranoia. You can make yourself sick with worry.*

In the Boardroom

1. **Greedy CEOs.** *I say amen to that!*

2. **Bankruptcy shenanigans.** Airlines that file bankruptcy, threaten to close down, slash employee paychecks and pensions, but then

quickly emerge from Chapter 11 and bid billions to buy another airline. Can you say US Airways? *I give another amen to that point!*

3. **Last-minute price gouging.** Just because the airline can take advantage of you when you're desperate doesn't mean they should.

4. **Overbooking.** In this day and time, why do airlines still overbook by 20 percent? If passengers don't show, they should lose all or most of the ticket price—period!

In the Break Room

1. **Airline unions.** They only give the right for employees to maintain snotty attitudes. *I don't agree, but I won't comment further.*

2. **Airline employees** who won't take responsibility and pass the blame elsewhere. *Well, speaking as an airline employee myself, most problems really aren't my fault. Blame management!*

People Skills

1. **The airlines' ever-diminishing concern for customer service.** Similar responses included: the cattle-car mentality, putting computers and/or incompetent personnel in charge of customer relations, the focus on the bottom line instead of the customer, and airlines that make promises and don't deliver. *Customer service was the number two complaint overall.*

2. **Rudeness.** "When did higher security mean the removal of courtesy?" asks one reader. No other customer-service business in this country could survive treating its customers with so much rudeness. This is mainly ground-based and very little follows through to the onboard portion of the industry. Sure, ground support puts up with a great deal of, shall we say, "difficult" customers, but that must go with the job. If the employees cannot handle or are not fit to handle difficult customers, then maybe this is not the industry

for them to work in. *While I somewhat agree, it is always good to practice putting the shoe on the other foot.*

People Themselves

1. **No dress code.** Would it be asking too much for people to cover at least 25 percent of their bodies? *No, thinking of the recent Southwest miniskirt episode.*

2. **Smoking—pro and con.** Antismoking activists and unrepentant smokers both chimed in on airport smoking policies. *Both made the list, but I just don't see smoking as much of an issue anymore.*

3. **Air travel advice givers.** *I'm thinking that would be yours truly, but I prefer to think that this reader meant Peter Greenberg, the so-called Travel Detective. It was only said once, but I got a good chuckle out of it so I thought I would include it.*

4. **Unrealistic expectations.** People who expect air travel to be way more than safe passage from point A to point B.

5. **People!** The airline world would be so much better without them. Obviously from burnt-out employees. Maybe they should work for the United Parcel Service or Federal Express.

Industry-Wide

1. **Environmental degradation.** Pollution, overdependence on oil, noise, waste, and non-recycling practices.

2. **Political correctness.** Traveling has become a sterile atmosphere, void of culture and personality with the airlines so afraid of offending someone. For goodness sake, is "Merry Christmas" so wrong to say? *Amen . . . oops!*

3. **U.S. airlines.** Many of you vented your frustration on particular airlines. Northwest got the most votes, but American, Continental, Delta, United, and US Airways all made the list.

4. **Unnecessary paperwork.** How many trees do we have to cut down to produce the millions of daily landing documents that are ignored anyway?

The variety of things that bother people about air travel never ceases to amaze me. Some of the bizarre comments included: too many choices, smelly feet, irritating pilot announcements, color schemes, employees who are liars, and, incredibly enough, the airplanes themselves. Call me crazy, but I think you need airplanes for air travel, unless of course hot air balloons or zeppelins are coming back in style.

Surprisingly, a large portion of the e-mail I received thanked me for writing about the positive side of air travel. This gives me true hope. In fact, I believe most people look on the bright side, and I like that about people.

CHAPTER SEVEN

50 Tips From ... *You*

E arlier this year, I wrote a column giving 12 tips for a better flight. At the end, I asked for readers' tips. I received thousands of responses and many great tips. The tips varied from interesting and common-sense to creative and funny. Here are some of the best.

General Travel Advice

1. Make a note of where you parked your car at the airport. After a long trip, your memory will almost always fail you.

2. Dump that hard-sided carry-on. A soft-sided bag has some give, so it can be crammed into tight spaces, but a too-big hard case will have to be checked.

3. Put a unique marker on your suitcase so you can recognize it easily when it comes around on the baggage carousel. (Tip #2 in popularity)

4. If your neighbor won't stop talking, pretend to sleep.

5. Stock up on zip-top bags. You can use them for snacks, as doggy bags, and as leak-tight carriers, and to protect important documents.

6. Join the airline's frequent traveler club even if you don't plan to fly on that airline ever again. Before you know it, you will have enough points for a free trip or upgrade. (Tip #3)

7. Cross-pack. On a cruise once, I watched one poor woman run the ship in a bathrobe for days because the airline had lost her luggage. Had she cross-packed with her travel companion, she would have had half the clothes she needed for the week.

8. Eye masks! (Tip #4)

9. Never place any important document in the front seat pocket —especially not your passport!

10. When confronted with a particularly nasty passenger, say "God bless you!" loudly. It almost immediately simmers people down. (Author's note: I tried this on a flight and it worked very well.)

Health

11. Visit the restroom before boarding the plane.

12. Drink plenty of water, and bring your own bottled water if you prefer it. (Tip #1)

13. Dab a little antibacterial ointment in your nose to help protect you from the myriad airborne contaminants circulating in the cabin.

14. Wear shoes to the restroom. Bare feet and bad aim are an unpleasant combination.

15. Don't eat chili peppers for breakfast. (I don't know why, but I imagine it has to do with "Plop plop, fizz fizz.")

16. Take sanitary wipes or wet towels with you. You will always need to clean or disinfect something onboard.

17. Match each alcoholic beverage with at least two glasses of water.

18. Exercise and stretch. (I agree. If you exercise and stretch, you will have more energy, and you won't feel as beaten up after a long flight.)

19. If you are allergic to cats, bring allergy medication. Passengers often bring cats onboard or carry dander on their clothes.

20. Use saline spray. I used to routinely get colds and respiratory illnesses soon after a flight, but since I started using a saline spray a few years ago, I have not once become ill after flying.

21. Always, always check that there is a "barf bag" in the pocket in front of you. You might not get sick, but you never know about your seatmate.

Kids

22. Pack a small toy or a bag of Goldfish or cookies in your carry-on—not for yourself or your kids to eat, but to quiet the screaming kid three rows back. Works every time and costs only pennies.

23. Schedule your flight for the kids' naptime, and keep the kids awake by any means possible until you get on the plane. The flight is so much more relaxing for everyone when the kids sleep through it.

24. When kids are howling or staring at you from the seat in front of you, hand them a crayon and the sick bag with instructions to make a hand puppet.

25. Bring dollar bills, and if a kid starts kicking your seat from behind, bribe him with money. Tell him if he's good for the remainder of the flight, he'll get $5. Works like a charm.

Comfort

26. Dress in classy but comfortable clothing.

27. Wear comfortable slip-on shoes. (Tip #7)

28. Unless you are traveling with children, always ask for an exit-row seat. You'll get more legroom.

29. When choosing your seat, ask the customer service agent where she would sit.

30. Pack your favorite hot sauce. It can turn the worst in-flight or airport meal into a culinary delight.

31. Wear noise-canceling headphones. (Tip #5)

32. Ladies and gentlemen: Don't wear thong underwear. (Not that I would know, but I hear it has to do with uncomfortable creeping. Aren't the men's styles called "banana hammocks"?)

Mental Health

33. Forget how it used to be, and play by the new rules.

34. Arrive early. (Tip #6)

35. Practice patience, and be prepared to test it abundantly.

36. Remember that people are people: They have feelings just like you. They come from very different walks of life. Some don't like to talk, while others need someone to listen.

37. Bring or form a mental picture of your "happy place," be it that perfect sunset on your trip to the Bahamas or your special loved one. It will serve as a reminder of the good things in life.

38. Be the person you would most like to fly with.

    Note: I received quite a few drug suggestions, everything from prescription medications to over-the-counter sleeping aids. For liability reasons I won't list them, but I do question the few readers who recommended Viagra!

Entertainment

39. Bring a pen and paper. Write letters, keep a journal, or jot down ideas or to-do lists.

40. Listen to an audio book. It takes up more time than the in-flight movie, and is better exercise for your imagination.

41. Make up lives for your fellow passengers. Look around you: See that woman in the sweats, the one who looks tired, but eager? She works in an office all week and she has a bullying boss. She's flying to see someone she loves, and is confident that he loves her, so she can wear sweats and be comfortable, because this weekend is all about comfort.

42. Books! (I was scolded many times by my readers for not including this tip. After all, I'm a writer myself. So, now that you mention it, you should bring one of my books!)

Humorous

43. Put your favorite wine in a water bottle so you don't have to pay the outrageous price for the onboard wine that tastes like cat pee.

44. Be nice to the check-in staff; it's not their fault airlines are inherently evil. (This is one of my favorites.)

45. For those who hate conversing with the total stranger in the next seat: Wear a button that says, "I'm not being rude, I'm ignoring you."

46. Ladies: Take the batteries out of your personal massagers; otherwise, the security search could prove quite embarrassing.

47. If you are from a particularly gassy family, don't eat cabbage or drink Hefeweizen beer before flying. Trust me on this!

48. Have great sex the night before you fly. You will be in a better mood and be more likely to sleep on the airplane.

49. Hire your own jet and pilot (nice for some).

50. Drive instead!

CHAPTER EIGHT

Carry On!

Airport carry-on rules don't make much sense. One moment there is a proposal to lift the ban on scissors, knives and, yes, ice picks, and the next moment, a ban on liquids is imposed. Huh? Do you find yourself confused? Do you have any idea what you can take on-board the plane? Well, I am a flight attendant and I am just as bewildered. But let me wade in here with some tips and maybe an occasional rant.

Mind you, I have rewritten this chapter several times just to keep current with the latest Transportation Security Administration (TSA) guidelines, so you'd better double-check the rules before you go (www. tsa.gov), because they have probably changed since I put down my pen.

But first let me ask you something. Have you noticed anything different about air travel recently? I mean, besides the hassle of checking your bags and waiting for them at the other end? Something inside the airplane? Why, yes. It's the sudden availability of space in the overhead compartments—even on full flights. It sure saves a lot of aggravation in my job. I think the last time flight attendants got a break like this was when smoking was banned on the airplane in the early 1990s.

I know it's pathetic to get excited over something so trivial, but surely nobody misses those gate delays caused by all those "carry-on" items. How many times did you get to your seat and discover—surprise!—the overhead bin was crammed tight with duffle bags, overnighters, laptops, shopping bags, Stetson hats, and coats of all shapes and sizes? You were then forced to stuff your carry-on under the seat in front of you, leaving no room for the items you'd most like to stow: your legs.

At the height of the London bomb scare, I worked up a trip to England just to see what it was like to fly with a total ban on carry-on items. Flight attendants seemed to dance through the aisles as they closed the overhead bins. A delightful hollow ring echoed up and down the cabin. OK, it was offset a bit by the grumpy passengers but, hey, the crew members had to check their bags, too.

Honestly now, how many of you have tried to de-liquefy your bags and still live your life as a clean and civilized human being? You know, change your roll-on antiperspirant to dry, leave the perfume and cologne at home, and, yes, actually use the dreaded hotel shampoo and conditioner? I attempted it on a quick trip to Seattle, and I ended up cutting myself multiple times (from shaving with soap and water) and smelling like a putrid almond (from the complimentary lotion).

Recently, authorities have modified the ban on liquids, and I am glad of that. Here are some important things you should know.

1. Travelers may now carry through security checkpoints travel-size toiletries (3 ounces or less) that fit comfortably in one quart-size, clear plastic, zip-top bag. At the checkpoint, travelers will be asked to remove the zip-top bag of liquids from their carry-on and place it in a bin or on the conveyor belt. X-raying the liquids separately will allow TSA security officers to more easily examine them.

2. Larger amounts of prescription liquid medications, baby formula, and diabetic glucose treatments must be declared at the checkpoint and are subject to additional screening.

3. After clearing security, travelers can now bring on-board beverages and other items purchased in the secure boarding area.

In other words, you can't bring your own bottled water from home. Okay, that makes sense. But then shouldn't there be a cap on how much vendors can charge for it? I will drink tap water before I will pay more than $5 for a bottle of water. Don't laugh. Once in a hotel room overseas I found a bottle of water with a price tag of $13.50 sitting next to a bottle of red wine selling for $6.50. I gritted my teeth and drank the wine. I am a man of principles, you know.

Here's one last rant, then the tips. Does it make anyone else mad to follow the carry-on rules, only to find yourself sharing a flight with Mr. Last Minute, who comes dragging what looks to be 13 carry-on bags? Actually, I don't get mad, I just don't help. And another thing: Why is there a weight limit for checked luggage but not for carry-ons? Doesn't this policy just encourage fliers to put their heaviest items in their cabin bags, making them even more dangerous if they fall out of the overhead bin?

My mother used to be one of the biggest offenders. Her excuse was that she had to fly standby (courtesy of free passes from yours truly) so she couldn't check her bags. She would always pack a minimum amount of clothing (all of it black because it went with everything, including black), but she is an avid book collector, and she kept dragging whole shelves of books aboard. On one trip she actually threw her back out trying to get the books home. I have since taught her to embrace the check-in process.

Did I say that was the last rant? Oh, well, here's one more. If the rules continue to force travelers to check their bags, then I hope the airlines will make it easier on their customers by assigning more staff to the check-in process. During busy times at an international airport it can take up to two hours in some of these lines—and I'm not even counting the wait at security.

Here are some quick carry-on tips:

1. Know when your bag is too big to carry on and check that big boy in.

2. Get a rollerboard suitcase that fits easily into the overhead bin lengthwise.

3. Make sure the bin shuts after you've stowed your bag. Your carry-on may be the first one in, but if it is protruding when the flight attendant checks the bin before take-off, it will be the first one yanked.

4. Use a soft-sided bag with some give to it. Hard cases can't be stuffed in tight spaces no matter how much you shove.

5. Baggage space disappears quickly on an airplane, so board as early as you can.

6. For safety and security reasons, try to use an overhead bin in your immediate area. It doesn't have to be directly overhead, but you should be able to see it from your seat.

7. When opening an overhead bin, always put your hand up, ready to catch anything that might drop out.

8. Don't worry if your carry-on gets yanked at the gate because of space limitations. Yes, you will have to check it, but it is pretty much guaranteed to be on that flight, and it will probably be the first bag out at baggage claim.

9. If you have something in your bag that you do not wish the security personnel to see, put it in your checked luggage. Trust me on this one.

10. Lend a hand to those in need, especially mothers, and don't get too mad at those who abuse the carry-on policy. Let them amuse you instead, but be sure to duck if they park their stuff over your head.

I hope this helps. As the days go by and the restrictions are eased, the overhead bins have filled up again, but it was good while it lasted.

See you on-board. Please, leave your ice picks at home. Luckily, TSA still prohibits this item!

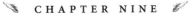

CHAPTER NINE

The Safety Demo: Theater of the Absurd?

A h, the safety demo—the announcement at the start of every flight that tells us what to do in case of a midair emergency. The words and props are familiar to every air traveler, but when was the last time you paid close attention? As a flight attendant, I can tell you the safety demo has some odd moments. The script is strange and the props are peculiar. While I am not underplaying the importance of the safety briefing, I suggest we take a humorous look at some of the quirkier features of the message and its delivery.

1. **Delivery.** There are several different approaches to the safety announcement. Some airlines jazz it up with celebrity impersonations, and others turn it into a comedy routine. Given a choice, most flight attendants will go for the no-nonsense delivery, but

sometimes a flight attendant will give a more dramatic reading or even embellish the script to get passengers' attention. For example:

- *The cutesy approach.* There may be 50 ways to leave your lover but there are only eight ways to leave this airplane, so please listen as we explain the safety features. Funny at first, but then I start to wonder: Will this flight attendant still be making jokes as we crash-land?

- *The scare-you approach.* "We will be traveling in this cylindrical tube full of flammable liquid five miles in the air and at over 500 miles per hour, so listen up." Okay, now I am too busy worrying about my last will and testament to listen to the safety procedures. I say, just stick to the script.

2. **Safety cards.** In the seat-back pocket is a safety card that says this: If you are unable to read these instructions, please notify a flight attendant. So, let me get this straight. If you can't read the card, you should tell me? But if you can't read the card, how would you know to tell me? Oh yeah, from reading the safety card!

3. **Stowage instructions.** Detachable wheels, also known as wheelies, should go under the seat in front of you and not in the overhead bin. Does anyone use these detachable wheelies anymore? I haven't seen a pair in years.

4. **The seat belt.** If you have ever been in an automobile in your life you should know how to use a seat belt. But on every flight we demonstrate how to insert the metal buckle, how to pull the loose end to tighten the strap, and then how to release the buckle. What if we just ask you to please fasten your seat belt and then offer you help if you need it? After saying all this, I must admit I once did have a passenger tie his seat belt in a bow.

5. **High-tech warnings.** Any electronic device using cellular technology should remain off for the duration of the flight. How do the flight attendants know if the transmit function has been turned on? Simple. We don't.

6. **Emergency-row exits.** Before your flight leaves, a flight attendant gives a separate briefing to the passengers sitting in the exit rows, informing them of their responsibilities and assessing whether they are physically capable of opening the door or window exit in an emergency. So far, so good. But have you ever taken a hard look at the people sitting in these seats? I have had 80-year-old ladies accept the assignment, not to mention people so huge they would never fit through a window exit, as well as passengers who can barely speak English. But flight attendants can't discriminate, so these folks can serve as your emergency helpers if they want to. They just have to be over a certain age, not handicapped and able to say "Yes" at the end of my little talk.

7. **Water landing.** "In the unlikely even of a water landing . . ." A water landing? Don't you mean a crash?

8. **Flotation.** "Your seat cushion can be used for flotation purposes." Really? You mean that uncomfortable, fart-infested cushion that hasn't been washed in years could actually save my life? Who would have thought?

9. **Life vests.** "In an emergency, inflate only one chamber of the vest upon leaving the aircraft." Real-life studies show that nine out of 10 passengers suffer from premature inflation, so don't worry if it happens to you. It's very common.

10. **Slides.** "Make sure you jump into the slide with your legs in front of you." Why in the world would you jump into anything with your legs behind you?

11. **The oxygen mask.** "In the event that it becomes necessary, oxygen masks will drop from the compartment above your seat. Be seated immediately, put on the nearest mask and breathe normally." Well, if that mask drops, here's what I'm thinking: I am five miles up in the sky and something is really wrong. "Breathing normally" probably isn't in the cards, but soiling myself might be.

12. **Final safety check.** "The flight attendants are now performing their final safety checks. If you have any questions about safety or security before we take off, feel free to ask them at this time."

Next time you hear this, be sure to ask this question and watch the flight attendant squirm: "The announcement says the bag on the oxygen mask does not inflate but oxygen is flowing to the mask, so why doesn't the bag inflate?" It got me the first time I was asked.

13. **The sign-off.** "Thank you for your attention." Well, the problem I have with this remark is that I am thanking people for something they have no control over. And if they weren't paying attention they wouldn't hear me say it, anyway.

In fact, many people ignore the safety demo, and some just pretend to pay attention. Only a few people listen intently. To those smart people, I really do say thank you. To those know-it-alls who decide to talk loudly during the safety demonstration, I have something different to say: Put a cork in it. People are entitled to hear the emergency information. It can, in fact, save your life.

CHAPTER TEN

10 Ways to Keep Cool While Flying

I t wasn't that long ago that we were complaining about the brutally cold winter that caused endless delays and cancellations. Now we find ourselves in the grip of the hot stale air of summer. The airports are packed with vacationing tourists, and things are literally heating up. Some people are starting to lose it.

The other day, there was a big commotion at a gate where the air conditioning system was broken. A group of passengers decided to protest by taking off most of their clothes. Police rushed in to contain the situation. I was one of the curious bystanders. To my dismay, the protesters turned out to be a group of rather large, elderly European travelers. Certain fantasies never quite work out the way you picture them in your mind.

Anyway, you don't have to take off your clothes to beat the heat. Here are my top 10 tips for keeping cool as you travel by air this summer.

1. **Take a jacket or sweater.** I know this sounds bizarre, but after sweating in the airport, in the jetway, and then on the plane before takeoff, you will freeze once you get airborne. That's when we blast the air conditioning. Moments later, your perspiration will turn to icicles. Trust me on this.

2. **Be the early bird.** If you get to the airport early, you'll have fewer worries, hurry less, and not sweat as much. Have you ever seen a fellow passenger so stressed out that he was practically raining perspiration? It's kind of amusing until you realize that he'll be sitting next to you.

3. **Tell a flight attendant.** If you are on the airplane and you're hot (or cold, for that matter), let a flight attendant know. Don't assume we already know. We move around the airplane so much that we generate our own heat, or we might be keeping cool by standing next to the air vents.

4. **Take a shower.** Many airports now have shower facilities. It's a great way to refresh and revitalize between trips. Not long ago, I was a passing through London on the way home from Barcelona. I paid 15 pounds ($23) for a shower and felt like a million bucks afterwards. They even ironed my clothes. Ask at an information desk if your airport has such an amenity.

5. **Crash the gate.** If you are at a gate where the air conditioning system is broken and you have plenty of time before your next flight, move to a cooler area. Many people think they have to stay by their gate, but you don't. Relief could be at the next gate over.

6. **Dress in layers.** When you get too hot, you can peel off some layers; when you're too cool, you can put them back on.

7. **Board last.** The number-one hot spot is the jetway. There's no air conditioning, and most of the time you're stuck in a long line that barely moves. If you don't need to board early to grab an overhead bin, stay in the cool gate area and wait until the gate agent announces the final boarding call.

8. **Leave more than enough time between flights.** Don't be the person running through the airport on a tight connection. Your seat partner will thank you, and your chances of getting a chill from the sudden temperature change are decreased tremendously.

9. **Don't stand for it.** Complain. And don't take "We are aware of the problem" for an answer. Now that airlines are cutting costs, they are less willing to provide supplemental air. If you threaten to walk off a flight or demand medical assistance, they will quickly pay attention to your needs.

10. **Practice good hygiene.** Don't be one of the smelly ones. Bring along adequate deodorant and use it. I was mortified one summer when I commented to my wife that somebody on-board had really bad BO. She replied, "Yeah, I think it's you." It can happen to anybody—even you.

11. I used to suggest **freezing water in bottles** and taking them with you aboard the airplane as cold water bottles, but this is not allowed under the new safety regulations. However, you are permitted to take an empty hot water bottle and fill it with ice at one of the fast food joints inside the terminal. Cold water bottles can be a great relief from that brutal heat and broken airport air conditioning system.

Hope this helps. Don't sweat it, and have a nice summer. Keep cool!

CHAPTER ELEVEN

Sick Flight? 6 Remedies

A irplanes are hotbeds for illness. Let's face it, the skies are getting cheaper and therefore more crowded. The more people you come into contact with, the better your chances of catching something nasty. Add the dry cabin air and toxic substances like hydraulic fluids, de-icing solutions, and pesticides, then mix in the cold-and-flu season, and you have the ingredients for a Go-Straight-to Bed cocktail.

Part of the problem may be the airlines' practice of mixing recirculated air with fresh air, a moneysaving move that was instituted in the 1980s. It is true that the recirculated air goes through a filtration system, but I can't say that I am over-confident about the filters' effectiveness. If they are so effective, why is that when someone in the front of a 747 does her nails, I can immediately smell the nail polish in the very back of the airplane? And why does the *New England Journal of Medicine* say that travel on airplanes has been found responsible for the spread of SARS? That doesn't sound effective enough to me. Don't get sick when you fly. Here's how to avoid the worst of it.

1. **Come prepared.** A cold can creep up on you during a multi-hour flight, so always bring a decongestant with you. This can also save you a painful landing by keeping your ears clear. Taking an herbal supplement containing echinacea before each flight can boost your immune system, and so can preparations that contain zinc. My potion of choice is Zicam.

2. **Use your fan.** If your seat partner has a case of the lung oysters, then turn on the fan above your seat. Point it towards you and to the side of your sick neighbor. Don't get into a deep conversation with him, and turn your head whenever he sneezes. Better yet, ask the flight attendant if you can switch to another seat. There is nothing worse than having sneeze hairspray applied to you every two minutes.

3. **Make a clean getaway.** Wash your hands every chance you get and try to keep them away from your face. It may help to remember that everything you touch on that airplane has been touched by at least 50 people before you.

4. **Layer it.** Dress in layers to keep your body temperature on an even keel. There is nothing worse than working up a sweat as you run through the airport for a connecting flight, only to wait on a freezing Jetway to board.

5. **Bring your own amenities.** Unless they are wrapped in plastic, avoid such on-board provisions as blankets, pillows, and headsets. Who knows what ailments afflicted the last person who used them.

6. **Sick? Don't fly!** If you have a cold, stay away from the airport. There is nothing worse than flying while battling to clear your ears, plus it is common courtesy to your fellow travelers to keep your germs to yourself.

Okay, you've taken your precautions, but you still end up getting sick—maybe even from your flight attendant. How many times have you boarded an aircraft only to be greeted by a flight attendant who is supposed to be smiling, but instead is blowing her nose? You cringe at the thought of taking a drink from her, much less getting within sneezing distance. But don't blame her; blame the airline's illness policy.

Flight attendants are exposed to many different people, germs, climate changes, and irregular hours. Flu, colds, and head lice are but a few of the maladies they contract as occupational hazards. Fortunately, flight attendants have provisions in their work rules that include paid sick time. But the airline industry is in financial trouble these days, and sick time increases operating losses. Solution? Management comes down on the employees, threatening disciplinary action for excessive sick leave. This policy scares junior employees into coming to work sick, and they in turn infect other employees and passengers. A chain reaction ensues and, before you know it, you have a mucous epidemic.

My advice to anyone encountering an obviously sick flight attendant is to get the flight attendant's name, then write the company and complain. The crew member will not get in trouble, but your complaint will send a signal to the airline to ease off on the sick-discipline issue. Also, refuse any drink or meal from anyone who is coughing or blowing. It is better to go hungry and thirsty for the duration of a plane ride than to be sick for a week.

I was able to stay off the sick list for 10 years with my current airline. One day my luck ran out and I caught the flu. I lay in bed, watched movies, sipped chicken soup, and slept countless hours—all the while getting paid. I decided to start work on a new home improvement scheme while recovering from the tail end of my illness.

In the hardware store, I saw something that horrified me: my inflight supervisor! Unfortunately, I was sure that he saw me as well. I dropped the bag of gravel I was holding and quickly spun around. I ran down the aisle and headed for the exit at the other end of the store, and to my dismay saw my supervisor doing the same. Was he following me?

The more I thought about it, the more ridiculous it became. I'm a grown man, and here I was running away from someone for fear of being scolded. I was still showing symptoms of my illness, but also knew that if I was well enough to be lifting heavy items in a home improvement store, I was probably fit enough to return to work.

After a sleepless night, I called and asked the secretary if I could speak to my supervisor. I felt I needed to explain myself.

"I am sorry," she said. "He has been on sick leave for the last few days. Can I take a message?"

I smiled, hung up the phone, and the matter was never spoken of again.

CHAPTER TWELVE

10 Tips for the Fearful Flyer

How many times have you boarded a flight and noticed one or two passengers who are acting a bit peculiar?

You might pass off the odd behavior as due to stress related to flying, reflecting a fear of flying. It becomes more evident as takeoff approaches. The wide eyes, clenched fists, profuse sweating, and rocking motions are among its symptoms.

I remember a middle-aged man who once boarded the aircraft, took his seat next to the window exit, and stuffed a rather large backpack under his seat. He smiled contently during the exit row briefing, and when we hit turbulence in-flight he clutched his backpack as if it were a teddy bear. But the smile never left his face.

When I asked him how he was, he told me that he used to be a fearful flier but had overcome his phobia. When I asked how, he told me that he carried a parachute on every flight.

Everyone has some degree of flying fear. You put yourself in a small cylindrical tube, loaded with flammable liquid, trust your life with some unseen pilot who, if media reports are to be believed, probably has a drinking problem. To make matters worse, you've been bombarded with graphic details of previous air fatalities.

Who wouldn't be scared?

Did you know that at least one out of every six adults has a fear of flying, also known as aviophobia or aerophobia? It is estimated that 35 percent of all airline crews, flight attendants, and pilots also have either a fear of heights or flying. We do this for a living, so don't worry if you have this fear too. The key is recognizing it and getting it under control.

The fear of flying has many different components, many of them stemming from other fears such as enclosed spaces, heights, strange sounds, sitting in stale air, crowded situations, lack of control, and the latest fear—terrorism.

Here are some statistics that may or may not be helpful.

1. Air travel is the second safest mode of mass transportation in the world. This is second only to the escalator and elevator. Your chances of being involved in an aircraft accident are approximately 1 in 11 million. Your chances of being killed in an automobile accident are 1 in 5,000. The most dangerous part of your flight is the drive to and from the airport.

2. All airplanes are designed and built to withstand far more stress than occurs in normal flight, including ordinary and extraordinary turbulence. The potential for damage to an aircraft is why flights will divert around or cancel due to thunderstorms.

3. 99% of turbulence injuries are from unfastened seat belts, or falling luggage from overhead bins.

4. You have more of a chance of dying from the food onboard than being involved in an aircraft accident.

Here are my top ten tips for the fearful flier:

1. **Don't conceal it.** Tell the gate agent when you check in, the flight attendant when you board, and the passengers around you when you sit down. It's nothing to be embarrassed about, and what you need is support, not added frustrations by suffering in silence. I make a special effort to check in on my fearful fliers several times during a flight.

2. **Treat the turbulence like bumps in the road.** Don't tense up or fight it, but, instead, let your body sway with the aircraft movements.

3. At check-in, **ask for a seat at the very front of the cabin** if possible. Turbulence is usually much greater in the back of the aircraft. If you have an extreme dread of flying, don't try to overcome your fears on a long flight. Take the shortest flight you can and preferably in the biggest plane possible.

4. **Keep distracted.** Watch the movie even if it's bad or you have seen it already. Read a book or do a crossword puzzle. Do anything that keeps your mind occupied and not dwelling on morbid possibilities.

5. **There are various classes** for those who are afraid to fly. In some cases the final test is an actual airplane flight. Try these websites:

   www.fearofflying.com
   www.fearless-flight.com
   www.fearofflyingdoctor.com/live_seminar.htm

6. **Avoid coffee or other caffeinated beverages**, since an overly hyper state of mind will only exacerbate your anxiety. But drink other liquids, as dehydration only contributes to the fear process. Some people recommend a glass of wine to calm the nerves, but don't overdo it.

7. **Listen to peaceful and calming music.** Your mind tends to wander and hear sounds that either don't exist or are perfectly normal flight noises.

8. **Try the "rubber band" technique:** Wear a rubber band around your wrist and if you feel yourself becoming agitated, snap the

rubber band against your skin. Apparently, the pain is a reality bite and takes the mind off the turbulence.

9. **Avoid thinking about gory details.** When an air disaster does occur, avoid the graphic details and overplay in the news media. It is important to be informed, but too much is too much.

10. **Breathe deeply as often as you can,** and remember that the sick bag in front of you can be used as an anti-hyperventilating device as well.

There is a free self-help audio assistance program that can be purchased and taken onboard with you. I have not heard it myself, but quite a few passengers I know swear by its effectiveness. For more information, go to www.fearofflyinghelp.com.

For obvious reasons, there are quite a few more fearful fliers in America now than there were before 9/11. I have seen and dealt with some of the more serious cases on-board—crying, screaming, loss of bladder and bowel control, tremors, pulled muscles from tension, and broken fingers and fingernails from gripping the armrest too tightly.

The inspiration to write about this subject came while flying in extreme turbulence. A female passenger started screaming at the top of her lungs, "We're all going to die, make it stop, make it stop!" This set off two other fearful fliers, where a man broke out in hysterical tears and another female yelled back, "No we're not, no we're not, somebody kill her now!"

Fear is the number one enemy. Kind of like during a heart attack, the fear of dying only makes the situation worse. I guess the saying is true, *"You have nothing to fear, but fear itself."* So accept your fear, treat it with common sense, and please leave your parachute at home.

CHAPTER THIRTEEN

Airline Coffee: A Bitter Cup, Indeed

J ava, Joe, morning juice, black gold, an ex-junkie's last vice—whatever you want to call it, coffee has a firm grip on this country's morning routine. The proof is in the long lines at the airport coffee stands every morning.

Coffee is served on airplanes, too, and it might even be supplied by that familiar purveyor of gourmet coffee from Seattle. Yet, sad to say, when you start to sip this coffee on an airplane, the only special taste you experience is that of a compost heap. How is it possible to screw up a cup of coffee so badly? I have several theories, all grounds (no pun intended!) for consideration.

1. **If the coffee is bad, you won't want a second cup.** I'm not saying that all flight attendants are looking to lighten their load, but

if the plane is oversold and understaffed, the last thing the flight attendant wants is extra requests for coffee. So, it's possible your crew is not being especially careful about making good coffee and keeping it fresh. In fact, I see this kind of "benign neglect" all the time.

2. **If the coffee is bad, folks will buy more at the airport.** Here's an interesting coincidence: The coffee you drink on the plane is often supplied by the same company that sells it to you in the airport terminal for $5 dollars a shot. Call me a conspiracy theorist, but if they sell an inferior blend to the airlines, then travelers might buy a cup in the terminal instead. Seattle gets the money both ways. Sounds like a brilliant business model to me.

3. **It's all in the H$_2$O.** Bad coffee starts with bad water. It is certainly true that airplane water doesn't taste all that great. It is, after all, from the local municipal water supply, and it's been sitting in the plane's water tank for a while. Bottled water makes much better coffee. If you don't believe me, next time you're in a hotel, pour bottled water into your room's coffeemaker. Even those wretched hotel coffee packets can turn out decent coffee if the water is good.

4. **You're drinking decaf—whether you want it or not.** Many flight attendants brew only decaffeinated coffee. Are they concerned about your jangled nerves? Not particularly. It's just that they'd rather have sleeping passengers than a hyperactive crowd any day. I am not condoning it; I'm just saying it happens. Did you know that airline coffee used to be 90% caffeine-free anyway? And did you know that a few airlines still serve mostly decaffeinated coffee as a matter of course?

5. **The water's not hot enough.** Some people say that airline coffee is bland because the water doesn't get hot enough to steep the coffee grounds properly. This theory doesn't make much sense to me, as I have been scalded by hot water plenty of times when I've been working in the galley.

Whatever the reason, most airplane coffee is pretty awful. So, what can you do about it? Here are some tips:

1. **Skip the cart.** Don't drink the coffee from the beverage cart. By the time it gets to you, the coffee is either cold or stale, and it's probably decaffeinated anyway.

2. **Make inquiries.** Politely ask the flight attendant's opinion of the coffee. If he frowns, take the hint. Sometimes he'll come back with a fresh pot for you later.

3. **Take a stand.** Get up and take a walk to the back of the airplane after the beverage service, and ask for a cup of coffee. The flight attendants will have time to brew it and you can see that the coffee is fresh.

4. **Tell a fib**. If you need a caffeine dose and you are in doubt as to what is being served, tell the flight attendant that you can't drink decaffeinated coffee, and you will get the right stuff.

5. **Have some taste.** If you don't take your coffee black, you might want to bring a favorite flavored creamer with you. Most of the time, the airlines have only ice-cold 2% milk to offer.

6. **Splurge.** Buy a cup of coffee before you get on the airplane, especially if it's early morning. Your first cup of the day should be the best—and exactly the way you want it.

7. **Spice it up.** Add some Irish cream to your coffee. I've never had a bad Bailey's coffee. If you want to skip the booze, there is a non-alcoholic flavored Bailey's creamer.

8. **Drink tea.** There aren't many ways to foul up a cup of tea.

One more tip: When the flight attendant asks you how you take your coffee, skip the jokes. We have heard almost every one of them (and let me tell you, some of them are quite crude).

While I am complaining about coffee matters, whatever happened to the "drip line" at coffee stands? You know: one line for specialty coffees and another (much faster) line for straight java. Believe it or not, there are folks who just want a plain cup of coffee and not some flaming macchiato nonfat cinnamon decaf latte with extra foam. I'm one of those simple people, and I have to wait forever in the long line just to tell the coffee "barista" that I am a drip, and, boy, do I feel like one by that time!

I used to be hooked on coffee. It was what I looked forward to most in the morning. I couldn't imagine my life without coffee until I became seriously ill from something I had eaten in South America. The doctor told me that I had to take three months off from alcohol ("easy," I mused), fatty foods ("piece of cake"), and caffeine ("oh no, he couldn't mean . . . coffee!")—especially coffee.

Well, after three days of "venti" sized headaches, I broke the caffeine addiction and turned into one of those decaf freaks that I used to make fun of. Ah, how the coffee table has turned.

CHAPTER FOURTEEN

Food for Thought

A ir travelers used to complain about how awful the food was at 35,000 feet. These days they complain that they get nothing at all. And it's true, you don't—not unless you're willing to fork over 10 bucks or bring your own sandwich aboard. How did it come to this? Money troubles, that's how.

SkySnax, BOB (Buy On-Board), SkyKitchen, Food for Purchase—the airlines have lots of words for it, but they all mean that complimentary in-flight meals are disappearing. They're already gone on most domestic flights, and they're getting harder to find on international flights. You can bet they won't be back soon. The airlines are financially strapped and are doing everything they can to stem the hemorrhage of money that is so prevalent now in the industry.

There are two ways to look at it:

1. **Outrage and indignation.** The airlines have hit a new low—they're charging for every little item. It's way out of hand when you can get on a six-hour flight, have no U.S. currency in your wallet, and listen to your stomach rumble from New York all the way to San Francisco.

2. **Optimism and opportunity.** Airline meals were never any good, anyway. At least now you have options: bring your own, buy at the airport or purchase onboard. Before, you paid for the food whether you liked it or not; it was lumped into the ticket price.

I recently flew from Chicago to Hawaii on a "domestic" flight, so if I wanted a meal I had to buy it. Mind you, this is a nine-hour flight. If I had arrived late in Chicago carrying only my credit cards, I'd have spent a long, hungry flight dreaming of pineapple and poi. Why? Because most airlines take only cash for their in-flight meals. I would have ended up eating the seat cushion. I'm a flight attendant, so I know to carry cash, but there's some poor, hungry guy on every flight who doesn't know this.

In the past, when passengers would ask me, "Don't you feel embarrassed about how cheap the airlines are getting?," I would have answered an immediate "Yes," but recently I've had second thoughts. The passengers are paying less and less for their tickets, and the savings have to come from somewhere. The employees' salaries and pension benefits are already tapped out, and the executives' paychecks—well, that's another story.

Nevertheless, I felt embarrassed for the Hawaii-bound crew as they had to answer many times, "Yes, seriously, you have to buy the meal." Shouldn't there be some kind of time limit on no-meal flights, or at least a place to store the food you bring aboard? Just a thought.

Here are some tips for dealing with food on your next flight:

1. **BYO.** Bringing your own is much more pleasant than being forced to pay $10 for a box full of preservatives or a greasy burger.

2. **Cold hard cash.** Have a spare $20 tucked away in a corner of your wallet. Airlines don't always take credit cards. They often won't take foreign currency, either. The man sitting next to me on the flight to Hawaii had connected from an international flight with only a credit card and a pocket full of Euros. I traded some cash for his Euros and he was most grateful.

3. **Yes, we have no bananas.** Stay away from bananas or any other fruit that is easily squished or ripened by enclosed cases. Apples are the perfect travel companions because they contain natural sugars that will quell your hunger pains—and they are natural toothbrushes. Also, you will feel better after eating an apple than you will after wolfing down that Double Whopper.

4. **Go nutty.** Trail mix is another great travel companion, and it will last a long time in your suitcase. Most flight attendants I know keep a spare bag with them, as they could go the better part of 12 hours without a meal.

5. **Got milk?** If you are hungry but can't stand junk food, ask for a carton of milk or tomato juice. Either one will get you to your next fuel stop.

6. **Beg, borrow, but don't steal.** If you are stuck on a flight with no cash and you are unbearably hungry, reason with the flight attendants. They are hardly going to let you starve—I know I wouldn't.

7. **Expect the unexpected.** You may have only one connection to make, but if it is through an airport having a thunderstorm, you may be sitting on the taxiway longer than you expected. Plan ahead and have a back-up stash of food.

8. **Dieting and air travel don't mix.** Don't start a high-nutrition scheme or a weight-loss regime around any type of flight. It is difficult to maintain nutritious values while flying. And, believe it or not, the fatty foods that are readily available in the airport and in the air do serve a purpose: They provide short-term satisfaction and last you a long time.

Purchasing flight food is now a reality of air travel. I was recently on an Iberia flight from Barcelona to London where they weren't only charging for the food, but also for the drinks. I am talking water, coffee—everything. Let's hope it doesn't come to that over here, or before long, there will be coin-operated toilets and overhead bins. Forget I said that. I don't want to give management any ideas.

Caution: Water On-Board

You hear media reports on the dangers of tap water one moment, and the dangers of bottled water the next. The current alarm is about the water you get on-board when you fly. It's all about fear and scaring readers so they will read more. Well, there are good reasons to be afraid.

Here are the facts of the matter. Most airlines these days board only a limited supply of bottled water on each flight. The ratio of bottled water to tap available depends on where you sit.

- *First Class:* 100% bottled water
- *Business Class:* 50% bottled, 50% tap
- *Economy:* 25% bottled, 75% tap

The airlines say there isn't enough room on the airplane to stock bottled water for every passenger. With the disappearance of in-flight meals, one might imagine there'd be plenty of room for water, so maybe it has more to do with shrinking airline budgets.

The tap water comes form the water tank, which is filled before each flight with water from the local water supply. This is the water that is used for coffee, tea, the lavatory sink, and the pitcher on the beverage cart. It is regular old, run-of-the-mill tap water: the same treated H_2O that comes out of your faucets at home—but with a twist.

The twist is the holding tanks. Some recent, highly publicized tests have found high bacteria and fecal counts in those tanks. Other, less well-publicized tests show normal readings for contaminants, but ask any mechanic who has stripped down a water tank, and you'll hear that it is not a pretty sight.

I have been a flight attendant for 16 years, and I believe that there are legitimate concerns about water on-board. Here are some tips that might help.

1. **Don't go overboard.** Hydration is good, but over-hydration is wasteful. A one-liter bottle of water is sufficient for all flights under eight hours. Any more will have you drinking your neighbor's share and running to the not-so-sanitary lavatory all too often (but that is a whole other chapter).

2. **Tap it.** If you are in good health and are really thirsty, don't be afraid to drink tap water now and then. In fact, many doctors encourage their patients to drink tap water as a way of building up their immune systems. More complications arise from dehydration than drinking tap water, anyway.

3. **BYOB.** If you absolutely, positively have to have bottled water, then you'd better bring your own. I don't condone it, but sometimes flight attendants do refill water bottles from the tap. The crews call it "Galley Springs." Don't bother asking whether you're getting real mineral water; tap water has minerals in it, too, you know.

4. **Get bubbly.** Ask for sparkling mineral water. It is from a natural source and can be a refreshing change from regular water. And there's no chance of a tap-water substitution.

5. **Don't fool yourself.** If it's in a pitcher, it's from the tap. I have never seen a flight attendant pour bottled water into a pitcher. Lemonade and fruit punch mixes also get the tap-water treatment.

6. **Mix it up.** A nutritionist once told me that if I mixed water with one-quarter cranberry juice or apple juice, I would retain the water longer and receive more of the benefits. I don't know if that's true, but ever since I started doing it, I have had considerably less jet lag and have woken up feeling more energetic the next morning.

7. **International caveats.** Airlines fill their water tanks with local water, so be extra careful when you are in areas with known water problems. Stick with the bottled stuff and be vigilant. Even brush your teeth with it. In this particular case, a quick water fix is not worth a case of "Delhi belly" or "Montezuma's Revenge," believe me.

8. **Skip the coffee break.** Don't drink the coffee or tea on those international flights, either, as the water on-board doesn't reach the required temperature to kill off all the bacteria. Skip the ice cubes, too, as they may also have been made from contaminated water.

9. **Watch for cons.** Always examine the bottled water you buy in foreign countries. A while back, I watched some young boys in the Mumbai airport fill up used bottles from the airport faucets, then melt the plastic seals back in place so the bottles would appear to be unopened.

10. **Plan ahead.** It is 2 a.m. as I write this, and I am in a European hotel staring at a bottle of water priced at US$13. A fierce battle is being waged between my thirst and my cheap side.

As for me, I always drink tap water at home, but when I fly, it's bottled water or nothing. "Everything in moderation" is generally good advice, but if you fly all the time, as I do, you shouldn't subject yourself to the elements all the time.

All this water talk has made me incredibly thirsty, and my thirst has conquered my cheap side. I crack open the bottle of $13 water, but I pour it into a fancy red-wine glass. After all, the water is more expensive than most of the wines I drink.

Refreshing, no bouquet, and no taste whatsoever. Which is good, I guess.

Cheers!

The Right to Recline

once heard that 75 percent of all in-flight fights break out after one passenger reclines his seat into the tiny personal space of another. OK, I've also heard that 90 percent of all "statistics" are fabricated, but I tend to believe this one.

Here's how it usually happens.

A grumpy passenger, who is over 6 feet tall and has spent too much money on vacation, boards his return flight front to aft. He notices the First Class seats, then the smaller Business Class seats, and sighs as he struggles into his pint-sized Economy seat. He skews his long legs sideways, trying to suppress his irritation, and prays for an uneventful flight home. But shortly after take-off, the passenger in front of him reclines his seat practically into his lap. It's the last straw. After a couple of bumps on the invading seat back—some inadvertent, some deliber-ate—words get exchanged, and pretty soon there's an all-out brawl.

Who is right and who is wrong here?

Nobody knows. Certainly, the airlines are to blame for the ridicu-lous seat size, but when you ask what the rules are, you won't get a straight answer. Instead, what you get is the presumptive right to re-cline. After all, the airlines have provided the means to recline; indeed, they encourage it with the chipper announcement we have all come to dread: *"We invite you to sit back and enjoy the rest of the flight."*

One clever frequent flier has invented a solution to the passenger-in-your-lap problem. It's called the "Knee Defender," and it consists of two plastic clips that attach to your tray table, preventing the seat in front of you from reclining. The Knee Defender protects not only your knees, but also your drink and your laptop—common victims of a passenger's sudden decision to thrust his seat backward. It has several settings, so you can do a partial block, too—which is handy. After all, if the person in front of you can't recline his seat at all, he will probably get suspicious, but if he can only recline part way, you will probably get away with it.

Unfortunately, some airlines have forbidden the use of the Knee Defender on their airplanes. Here, then, are other tips to keep some stranger from reclining into your lap:

1. **Just say no.** If you fly often enough you will eventually notice that some seats don't recline. On most airplanes, these include the seats in front of the emergency exit and those in the very last row. When making your reservation or when you arrive at the gate, in-quire if your assigned seat is at one of those locations. If it is, don't accept it. Otherwise, everybody will be reclining except you.

2. **Make friends with the ticket and gate agents.** The ticket and gate agents know everything about the configuration of your airplane and the seat assignments for your flight. If you approach them in a courteous manner, they will often help you get a seat with little "squeeze factor."

3. **Sit elsewhere.** Many times passengers who get into fisticuffs over the right to recline could have avoided the fight altogether by sim-

ply moving to another seat. You're not required to sit in your assigned seat, you know.

4. **Straighten up.** While I am not letting the airlines off the hook on the tiny-seat issue, it is possible that your lack of legroom is due to bad posture. Sit up straight and notice how many inches you create for your legs.

5. **Be reasonable.** Before going ballistic at the passenger in front of you, take a look around. Most likely, the person in front of him has also reclined, and the inevitable chain reaction then took place. There is usually a happy medium in these matters; lean back a little yourself, and see if that's enough breathing room.

6. **Bump not.** If you decide to retaliate by bumping, kicking, or tapping the seat in front of you, all chances of reasoning will be lost and a scene will be that much closer.

7. **Plead hunger.** Most people understand that in order to eat your food, you need to be able to see it (sometimes it's better not to see the food, but that's a different topic). If the person in front of you refuses to return to an upright position, he risks getting chicken or beef dropped on his forehead. Not that you would do that intentionally, of course.

8. **Push that call button.** There may be fewer flight attendants in the cabin these days, but most of the time we are sympathetic to your plight and will try to assist in any way we can.

9. **Spend a penny.** Some airlines are now charging extra for economy seats with a few extra inches of legroom. If you have long legs, spend the money. Your comfort is worth it.

I have a friend who, when all else fails, just starts to sneeze. That usually gets the offending recliner upright in a hurry. But this unsanitary tactic could well set off an all-out conflict, so I don't endorse it. The same goes for pointing your overhead fan directly on the recliner's forehead, but I have to admit that I have done that a couple of times and it worked.

In the end, you have to put the shoe on the other foot. We live in a world in which tensions are already exacerbated by the volume of traffic, overpopulated neighborhoods, and obscenely long lines. We just have to learn to get along with one another in life—and that goes double on an airplane.

✎ CHAPTER SEVENTEEN ✎

Flying Large

I f we live in a world where the average person is getting taller and heavier, then why do the airlines continue to make their economy seats smaller and smaller? The obvious answer is that more seats generate more income. But whom do you feel more sorry for: the passenger who barely fits into his seat, or the passenger whose seat space is taken up by the spillage of body mass next to him?

For weight and balance purposes, the average airplane passenger was once assumed to weigh 165 pounds. After a few incidents, the Federal Aviation Administration upped the average to 190 pounds, but it seems the airlines are taking no notice of this change when it comes to seat comfort. And they won't, either—not so long as travelers choose their flights by price.

Southwest Airlines got blasted by the media a while back for requiring extra-large people to buy two seats. Right or wrong, at least
Southwest did something about the problem, instead of ignoring it or
hoping it would just go away. Most airlines still do not have a policy
addressing the large-passenger issue.

I am 6 feet 2 inches tall and weigh 195 pounds, and I have space
problems when I fly. Can you imagine what somebody twice my size
goes through? Big, bulky, plump, tall, obese, long-legged, big-boned
— whatever you call it, it adds up to trouble. Most people recognize
when they have size trouble, but here is a little guide in case you don't.
You have a size problem on an airplane when:

1. You can't put your tray table down all the way.

2. A flight attendant brings you a seat-belt extender without your
    asking.

3. You have to duck when boarding the airplane.

4. You have to fold your legs just to sit down.

5. Passengers can't see the overhead screen because your head is in
    the way.

6. You have to sit at an angle.

7. When you are sitting, more than 30 percent of your body hangs
    over into the aisle or seat next to you.

8. You barely fit through the lavatory door.

9. You seriously wonder if you would fit through the window exit.

10. Your seat neighbor can't see his armrest.

I find it tragic that on just about every flight, three large people are
wedged into one row while one smaller passenger is enjoying three
seats to herself. But since the airlines may not discriminate by size, and
computers do most of the seat planning, the big guys' bad luck just
continues.

Here are some tips for flying large more comfortably:

1. **Look it up.** Most airlines have good websites that detail the seat sizes and special facilities for each plane, and allow you to choose your own seat.

2. **Pick your seat.** Whether you are booking online, by phone or through a travel agent, reserve the right seat for you. If you're tall, a seat in the emergency exit row will give you more legroom. If you're bulky, a window seat will allow you more room to maneuver. If you're both tall and bulky, an aisle seat might be just the ticket. Explain your situation and make sure your request is typed into your booking comments. Get the booking confirmation number and carry it with you in case your requests are not met.

3. **Don't ask, don't get.** Ask the gate agent and the flight attendant for help getting the best seat for you. Most will try everything to accommodate you. If possible, ask a bigger crew member, as he will be more familiar with your plight.

4. **BYOB.** If you are a frequent flier and are tired of asking for a seatbelt extender, then bring your own. You can buy FAA-approved extender belts at many airport shops. Unlike the extenders used on a couple of airlines I know, these belts are not bright orange.

5. **Check the time.** Fly during off-peak hours. You are much more likely to find the adjacent seat unoccupied.

6. **Pay it forward.** Some airlines offer bigger seats with more legroom for a small additional charge. Don't be cheap; your comfort is worth the extra money. If you have bought two seats, be sure to tell the flight attendants so they won't try to move someone next to you.

7. **Move on.** If you see two seats free after the doors have closed, either move when you can or suggest kindly to your seat neighbor that he might be more comfortable with the extra arm room in the other seats.

8. **Rise to the occasion.** If possible, raise your armrest. You and your seat neighbor will both enjoy the couple of inches of space that becomes available.

9. **Board early.** When the agent makes the announcement for early boarding, go for it. You qualify, as you need extra time and assistance. This is also a good time to ask for a seat-belt extender or to explain your special needs.

10. **Last resort.** If you do not fit in your assigned seat and the flight is full, and if all other efforts have failed, then ask to take another flight. This action might inspire the gate agent or flight attendant to miraculously find you another seat, as they do not want to delay the flight by pulling your luggage out of the hold. This will also signal that you are serious about your problem and are not just trying to pull a fast one. But do this only as a last resort; otherwise, you might find yourself waiting for hours in the airport for the next flight.

One major airline got itself into a heap of legal trouble when its supplier of seat-belt extenders experienced a small design oversight. This item is generally classified as a "Technical Service Order" or TSO, and the Federal Aviation Administration is often abbreviated as FAA. Since the supplier printed FAA on one side of the belt and TSO on the other, when it was buckled it read FAATSO. By the time the problem was spotted, the supplier had already manufactured several thousand extenders, so I guess you could say it was a BIG problem.

If you are a passenger who is sitting next to someone who is overflowing into your seat, you too have rights. You can use some of the above tips yourself, but please do so as courteously and sympathetically as possible. There is nothing worse than making a scene with a large seatmate and then having to sit next to that person for hours on end. I warn you, I have seen this happen many times, and it is never pretty. If everyone would just practice common courtesy, flying could be a happy adventure for all of us.

Lap of Luxury

In an effort to win back high-revenue passengers, some airlines are investing hundreds of millions of dollars in new, First Class seats that can be transformed into offices, media centers and flat comfort beds. And while I have enjoyed using these futuristic seats on international flights, I also have a few problems with them.

1. As the First Class seats get ridiculously bigger, the Economy seats just get smaller. It's like a modern-day Robin Hood, only backwards: stealing from the poor and giving to the rich. I was in an Economy seat the other day and was so cramped that I could barely open up my laptop. The seat in front of me was reclined into my lap, my arms had no leeway to type, and my knees were

wedged against the tray table. Come on! Only so many sardines can fit into the tin.

2. The new First Class seats have control panels that rival the ones in the flight deck. They control the VCR, the rotating lumbar support, the noise-cancellation headsets, the privacy screens, the laptop power sources, the mood lighting, the video-on-demand, the video games, and much more. Some airlines train their flight attendants on the basic functions, but most don't. Have you ever asked your flight attendant what some button or switch was for, or how it worked, only to hear, "I don't know"? I have not only seen it, I've said it myself once or twice. A young male passenger with a frightened look on his face once asked me what the "Eject" button was for. I explained it was for the VCR, not for unruly passengers—but what a good idea!

3. With more functions comes the inevitability of more breakdowns. The airline mechanic is not trained to fix the new seats, and while we wait months for the manufacturer to send a repairman, they go out broken flight after flight. There is nothing worse than getting a broken seat in First Class. You feel ripped off, especially if you feel that you are paying way too much for your ticket to start with.

4. Even though the airline industry just came out of a gigantic financial crisis and had to slash the paychecks of its frontline employees, millions of dollars are going into these seats. So where did all the money come from all of a sudden? Oh yeah, I guess from my paycheck.

5. Here is another question: With all this fancy technology, why can't U.S. carriers offer in-flight Internet access? After all, many international carriers offer plug-in and wireless access. And while I am on the subject of computers, what's the deal with all these different types of power cords? This one works with Sony computers but not with Gateways, or that one works on Delta but not on American. Would it be so hard to just put plugs at the seats? Oh, but wait, that technology is already available—on foreign carriers. I recently flew on ANA, an Asian airline, and they had U.S. plugs

at every seat. I was embarrassed that my own country was falling so far behind. Can you imagine actually charging your iPod or answering your e-mail in-flight? It sounds too good to be true.

The other day, a passenger actually complained that his seat was too big. That was a first for me, but I can remember an in-flight occurrence that made me feel the same way. I was working a night flight to Europe, and my First Class passengers were fast asleep. The sun would be rising soon, so I decided to close all the window shades. But those First Class seats convert into beds, making it very difficult to reach the windows.

Improvising with a coat hanger, I managed to close most of the shades, but I lost my footing while closing the last one and landed in bed with a passenger—unfortunately, a very buxom woman. As I struggled to get to my feet, I grabbed the wrong leverage points. She woke up and started to scream, and all the passengers in the cabin instantly awoke in fear. There I was, face flushed, hair mussed, standing over an amply endowed, screaming woman with two buttons ripped off her blouse. How was I going to talk my way out of this one?

After profuse apologies, we regained our composure. I asked the woman and a female flight attendant to join me in the galley for a discussion. Luckily, the woman was an airline employee, and after I explained what had happened, she let me off the hook. She could tell by my demeanor that I was very distraught, and she half-heartedly laughed it off, although I sensed she still had her doubts. I can't say I blame her.

I wrote up a report just in case the misadventure developed into something bigger. I mean, what if this lady wasn't as understanding as she seemed to be? She had 12 First Class witnesses to an apparent grope-and-fondle.

What was I going to say? "The seat made me do it"?

The Air at 35,000 Feet

There was a time when the air on airplanes was truly awful, but the days of smoking in-flight are long gone. I know I am dating myself, but I remember passing out five packs of cigarettes to passengers in First Class; the flight attendants kept the leftovers for themselves. That was when smoking was considered sophisticated, and no one thought very hard about what was happening to their lungs.

Times changed, and smoking was relegated to the back of the airplane. But it was ridiculous to call 39A a nonsmoking seat when 40A was the start of the smoking section. The smoke would drift forward and enter the air system; by the end of the flight, everyone smelled like a cigarette butt. Soon smoking was sent packing.

You would think that with the departure of tobacco we all would be breathing a lot easier. But not so—at least according to some travelers.

Many people believe that recirculated cabin air deprives passengers of oxygen, spreads disease, and dries people out like prunes. Others believe that low oxygen levels on airplanes often cause hypoxia; affected passengers, they say, just don't recognize the symptoms. Of course, the airlines periodically conduct their own "scientific" studies, which uniformly conclude that cabin air is perfectly healthy.

Who's right? Let's consider a few common myths:

Myth: Pilots recycle the air and deprive the cabin of fresh oxygen in order to save fuel.

Fact: Well, yes and no. On newer airplanes, fans recirculate 50 percent of the cabin air, but fresh air is continuously pumped in from outside. Pilots do have the ability to turn off the fans and pump in only fresh air, but this is not standard operating procedure because it would consume too much fuel. Fresh air would improve the air quality in the cabin somewhat, but it would not raise the oxygen level.

Myth: The cabin air is drier now than it used to be.

Fact: Actually, the air is probably moister, but you're not going to like the reason. The recirculation of the cabin air raises the humidity level by taking in passengers' breath exhalations, sweat, sneezes, and other bodily effluvia. But I prefer not to think about that too much.

Myth: The cockpit has five times more oxygen than the cabin.

Fact: No. The oxygen level is the same throughout the plane at all times. The flight deck does receive a higher proportion of colder, outside air than the rest of the cabin; this is to compensate for the heat generated by the electronic equipment in the cockpit. Remember, oxygen level and air quality do not go hand in hand. The higher concentration of fresh air in the cockpit may make for a fresher environment for the pilots, but the oxygen level is no different from what you get in First Class or coach.

Myth: The airline never cleans the air filters and this spreads disease.

Fact: Actually, the air is quite healthy because of the High Efficiency Particulate Air (HEPA) filters, which can catch up to 99.9 percent of small bacteria and viruses (even SARS and bird flu viruses). The filters actually become more effective over time as trapped particles make it even more difficult for other matter to pass through. Nevertheless, the filters are replaced on a regular schedule; otherwise, a large buildup would reduce the flow of oxygen and cost the airline money. So, if you come down with a cold after a flight, don't blame the filters. Blame your sneezy seat neighbor.

Myth: The air quality is better in First Class and worse in the back of Economy.

Fact: This is actually true, and it is due to the design of the airplane. Oxygen comes in from the front of the airplane and exits out the rear in a system called FART (Forward Air, Return Tail). Quite ironic, but I won't go any further with that one.

Now, having said all of that, there are things to look out for and precautions to take to make sure the cabin air remains healthy and to keep the germs away.

1. **Count headaches.** If an unusually high number of your seat neighbors complain about headaches or dizziness, contact a flight attendant. Ask if others have the same symptoms, and if so, ask that the cockpit turn off the recirculation fans for a while. This won't increase the oxygen level, but it will improve the air quality.

2. **Turn on the vent.** In my experience, most people who complain about stale air do not have their vent turned on. You would be surprised what a little direct air can do for the mind and body.

3. **Wash up.** If you are afraid of catching a cold from your seat neighbor, make sure you wash your hands every chance you get and avoid touching your face. Better yet, bring antibacterial hand wipes along with you.

4. **Get ionized.** The new trend is to wear a small personal air ionizer around your neck. The device purportedly sends a stream of air-purifying ions up toward the nose. You might get some stares, but some people swear by these things. There is a popular belief that these devices create more pollution then eradicate.

5. **Hit the bottle.** If you are suffering from headache, nausea, confusion, or clammy skin, or if you are having difficulty breathing, ask a flight attendant for supplemental oxygen. Airlines are required to carry it and to dispense it at no charge.

6. **Bug out.** Some destinations require airline personnel to spray insecticide before landing. This is not an airline requirement but the destination's requirement, so don't get mad at the flight attendants. Instead, wet a handkerchief or, if you are well prepared, don a disposable surgical mask before they spray.

7. **Squelch the sneezers.** If someone is sneezing or coughing and not covering his mouth, don't be afraid to say something. Once I was flying standby and was afraid to speak up about a cougher. I ended the flight with hair full of phlegm and a weeklong cold.

8. **Don't obsess.** There is a businesswoman who is often on my flights. She is in her late 50s, conservatively dressed and very polite. Right before takeoff, she always puts on an elaborate hat made completely of aluminum foil. She doesn't laugh or make light of it; she believes the hat protects her from solar radiation. But, really, you don't need such a hat, and you shouldn't obsess about the air quality on the plane, either. Your stay on the airplane is brief, and the air you breathe is no more dangerous than the air in your workplace.

But people still have their worries, and commerce has ingeniously stepped forward to meet them, offering such products as special facemasks and personal filters that fit over the air vent above your seat. I have even seen oxygen bars at some airports. If I know the airline industry, it is busy concocting some way to charge you for the oxygen, too.

If only the airlines would start using some common sense. Now, that would be a breath of fresh air.

Hot Tips for Cold Flyers

A t the height of the winter season, the last thing you want to do is board an airplane (unless, of course, you are going somewhere warmer). You brave the snow and ice, endure the weather delay at the gate, then finally board the aircraft—only to freeze your rear end off.

You tell the flight attendant you are cold, but she just shrugs and says, "It feels all right to me." Or she agrees with you but does nothing. Hours pass. By the time you arrive at your destination, you've caught a chill and can no longer wiggle your toes.

If you're anything like me, you have a low tolerance for cold. I am a cold-feet person, and I'm not talking about being slightly chilled. By the time I get into bed, I have ice cubes for feet. One winter's night, I made the mistake of trying to warm my feet on my wife and woke up the next morning with a black eye from a retaliatory elbow. Now I recognize my affliction and take measures to deal with it properly.

There is an art to keeping warm on an airplane. I hope the following tips will keep you snug and cozy on your next flight.

1. **Be prepared.** Dress in several layers of clothing, preferably made from wool, cotton, or synthetic fleece. As you acclimate to the cabin, take off a layer at a time. This way you won't sweat, and if you need more warmth, you'll have a layer to put back on.

2. **Demand heat.** If the flight attendant doesn't turn up the heat, ask the people around you if they feel cold, too. Since the attendants are standing and moving around the cabin, they may not feel the chill as intensely (remember, heat rises), so they may not recognize the problem.

3. **Get up.** I know it's odd to hear a flight attendant tell you to leave your seat, but did you know that standing will increase your heat production by 20 percent? Walk around the cabin, stretch in the back of the airplane, or get yourself a cup of coffee or tea.

4. **Location, location, location**. If you are sensitive to cold, do not—and I repeat, do not—sit by an exit door, especially on a 757 or 767 aircraft. Sure, you will get extra legroom, but your feet will freeze and you will barely be able to feel them again. Fact: A man fell asleep on a five-hour flight next to an airplane door and woke up with frostbite on one of his toes.

5. **Pass on the Bud, Bud.** Skip the booze when the attendants come around with the drinks cart. Alcohol is tempting when you are cold, but it is dehydrating and may also suppress shivering, those involuntary muscle contractions through which the body warms itself.

6. **Hold the lemon.** Hot water with lemon sounds like the perfect concoction to erase your chill, but you will get it in a Styrofoam cup, which the lemon juice will cause to disintegrate. Now, I'm no doctor, but ingested Styrofoam can't be good for you. Brainstorm: Bring your Starbucks cup aboard and have the flight attendant fill that up.

7. **Toasty tootsies.** Get SmartWool socks. I never leave home without them in winter. They are made from a super-fine New Zealand wool that is heaven for your feet. I also endorse battery-operated socks. They are like an electric blanket for your feet. But don't put them on until after you get through security. You don't want the Transportation Security Administration thinking you're a sock bomber.

8. **Hottie-bottie.** This tip is pure genius and a favorite among flight attendants. After you finish your bottle of Evian, keep the container and ask the flight attendant if you can fill it up with a mixture of tap water and hot water from the coffee maker. After a few tries you will get the combination just right, and voila: an instant disposable hot-water bottle. It can be used as lumbar support, a sore-muscle reliever, or, if you are like me, as a glorious foot friend that will keep you warm the entire flight.

Don't let your air travel leave you cold this winter. Fly safe and fly warm.

Lavs and Lav Nots

O f all the airplane lavatory myths, the ones about the giant sucking sounds are the most . . . odorous.

For example, the intense whoosh emanating from the WC at cruising altitude is not the jettisoning of waste. It's the sound of a toilet delivering the cargo to its final destination: the septic tanks.

And no one has ever gotten stuck on the crapper because of the resulting vacuum. That's an urban legend. (Think about it—have you ever created an airtight seal around a toilet seat? Didn't think so.)

But, seriously, no one bothers to give much thought to the airline facilities. And I think they should.

I'd say the biggest problems with the lavs are the lines of people waiting to use them. There is what we call "rush hour traffic" for the toilets. Those times are: after take-off, after the meal, after the movies, and right before landing. Those would be the times to avoid—if humanly possible.

Here are 10 pieces of potty wisdom, collected from years of experience as a flight attendant.

1. If possible, use the restrooms in the airport terminal before you board an airplane. They are roomier, more modern, and a much better option than being forced to follow a big man holding a Sunday newspaper.

2. Wear something on your feet at all times. Men with a bad aim are all too common. I can't tell you how many people walk into these cubicles with bare feet. You may drink bottled water, eat low-fat meals, and keep in shape, but why would you walk around in sewage?

3. If you have been waiting a while and no one emerges, inform a flight attendant. Someone could be in trouble or, more likely, the flight attendant forgot to unlock it after take-off. I admit that I have done that a few times.

4. If one or more lavs are broken and lines are long, then the remaining restrooms become available to everyone. Ask the flight attendant to permit usage of restrooms in all service classes.

5. Avoid "rush hour" and the increasing agony of a protracted wait.

6. Do your thing and get out; people will be very thankful. Don't start a makeover or new book.

7. Check the seal between the door and the lock. I caught a little boy intensely staring into the door. When I investigated I found he was staring at a young woman removing her bodysuit. Be careful, this happens more than you think.

8. Obey the "fasten seat belt" sign, but—and I do mean butt—when you gotta go, you gotta go. Although we can not give you permission, we cannot stop you if you are insistent, and we sure don't want to spend the remainder of the flight dealing with your little accident on the seat.

9. Be courteous and think about the people behind you. If you made a mess, clean it up. At the very least, don't forget to flush. Every little bit helps.

10. If you are in the window seat and the people beside you get up, by all means do the same. Murphy's Law has it that if you don't, as soon as they sit back down, you will feel that urge.

I read the other day that one of the Asian airlines is planning to upgrade their First Class lavatories. This will include windows, soft lighting, and classical music. Why would any one want to ever come out? The lines will be astronomical, but I can just hear the publicity now:

"Come fly with us, it will be a truly moving experience."

Or how about:

*"Fly our airline, the only airline to provide you with a
'Poo with a View'."*

Whether we like it or not, with long flights come dirty toilets, because of bad aims, confusing toilet paper dispensers, and different notions of hygiene. It's bound to get a bit messy.

Flight attendants will attend to general tidying from time to time, and even on a couple of Asian airlines they have one crewmember whose main purpose is lavatory cleaning. Sounds good, right? But let's talk honestly, folks; do you want someone serving you lunch, who just got off of lav duty? Think about it.

Some female flight attendants pride themselves on the fact that they don't actually sit down on the toilet seat. They have perfected (almost) the art of hovering. So don't always blame the men for the bad aims. Pilots on some planes even demand a private restroom. I know many crewmembers who refuse to use the toilet for a certain bodily function, and one of them actually hurt herself by delaying the inevitable too long.

It's getting way out of hand. All you need to do is to wipe the seat thoroughly with a paper towel and then use a seat liner. Let's not get all blocked up over matters.

This is one necessary function that we all share. If we all approach this personal subject with a little humor and consideration, I guarantee that it will truly be a smoother move for all of us. (Pun intended.)

The In-Flight Movie

H ave you ever watched a movie on an airplane and thought the content was a bit inappropriate? Over the years, I've seen disaster movies like "Poseidon," "Titanic," "Air Force One," and I have even seen a movie about Pearl Harbor on a flight to Japan. What's next, "Snakes on a Plane"? "United 93"? I think a good rule of thumb for in-flight entertainment would be to avoid movies in which passengers die in a mass-transportation disaster. Same goes for the airport lounge. I still remember returning from my military service overseas, a long time ago. As I waited for my flight out of Frankfurt in the USO lounge, they played the old classic "Airport 75."

When the airlines stopped charging for in-flight movies, was it any surprise the selection got worse? I can remember once announcing our in-flight movie as "Cocoon: The Return," and being positive that I had seen it on television the night before.

And how many times have I had a flight full of businesspeople, and the only movie available was an animated flick aimed at children under 10? Who chooses these movies? Why not mix it up a bit and pick some movies that appeal to all ages, have received good reviews, and yet haven't already been seen by more than 100 million people? I'm sure there are plenty of them out there.

But then again, everyone's a critic, so it's lucky that many airplanes now have multi-channel video systems. The movie selection is more diverse, and you should be able to find something interesting to watch. Just be aware that many airlines do not censor or edit the movies they offer on their multichannel systems. I'm all in favor of minimal censorship provided the film's rating is clearly understood beforehand. The onboard personal video systems also play movies that have not been censored. When these systems were relatively new, some flight attendants would unwittingly play the uncensored videos on the main system. One showing of "Monster's Ball" was enough to change that.

Here are eight tips for getting the most out of your in-flight movie:

1. **Listen up.** Use your own headset. Many passengers board the airplane listening to personal stereos, but when it comes time to watch the movie, they reach for the airline's free headset in the seat-back pocket. Believe me, your headset is at least 10 times better and probably a whole lot cleaner.

2. **Unplug later.** A lot of people don't plug in the headset because they have too hastily decided they won't watch the movie ("I think I'll just finish this report/write my column/read this self-help book"). Of course, they then find themselves subconsciously watching the movie anyway. When they finally do plug in the headset, they've missed half the action and can't follow the plot. So, listen first and decide later whether you want to watch the movie or do something else.

3. **Turn down the lights.** If you're not enjoying the view outside and you are sitting next to the window, lower your window shade. It

will create a more movie-like atmosphere and improve everyone's viewing.

4. **Give it a shot.** If you haven't heard of the movie before and have nothing better to do, try it out. Some of the best movies I've ever seen are the ones I was unfamiliar with. Sometimes, when your expectations are nil, you get a pleasant surprise.

5. **Get some sleep.** For me, the best way to fall asleep on an airplane is to watch a bad movie. Halfway through, your mind wanders off into your own personal plot and pretty soon you're down for the count. Though this is common knowledge among flight crews, it doesn't pay to say so. One flight attendant got fired for announcing, "Today we have a movie that will surely put you to sleep." Unfortunately, the movie's screenplay writer was on that flight and he vigorously complained to management.

6. **Raise your hand.** If the movie starts at any point other than the beginning, let a crew member know immediately, as we will be busy doing other things and probably won't notice. On one flight, I started the movie at the end by mistake and nobody ever let me know. When asked, a few passengers said they thought it was a preview. Meanwhile, I had just ruined an exciting ending for everyone.

7. **Plan your break.** If you desperately have to go to the bathroom, don't wait until the end of the movie, as this is typically rush hour for the lavatories and you may find yourself in agony at the back of a lengthy line.

8. **Bring backup.** The electronics aisles are full of portable DVD players, laptop computers, and video iPods. If you don't like the onboard movie selection, take matters into your own hands.

Things have changed since the days of the two-tube headset, but with modern technology has come a host of new problems and interesting situations. Take live TV, for example. While this is a great thing, especially for must-see sports programs, how would you like to have been aboard the JetBlue flight whose passengers got to watch their own life-or-death drama on TV when the plane's landing gear failed to descend?

If I were preparing for an emergency landing, I wouldn't want to hear a news analyst discuss the worst-case scenario, would you?

Video games are great, too, but I am not so sure about them in-flight. Have you ever listened to two people play a combat game without the volume? It sounds like a bad porno movie. Sure, the players have their headsets on, but what the other passengers hear is something like, "No, no, no! Yeah, yeah, there ya go. Oh, that's it, just like that, OOOOOOOHHHHH!"

So maybe skip the video games. Next time, sit back, relax, and enjoy the in-flight movie, even if you've already seen it. It will pass the time and it will give your laptop solitaire or Sudoku skills a rest. Save those for your wait in the airport terminal, when you will really need them.

Baby On-Board

T here I was, baby in one hand, diaper bag in the other, at the gate, paralyzed by indecision. The gate agent had inquired if I wanted to upgrade to First Class.

I was haunted by my own demons, having written an article a couple of years earlier about the evils of letting infants fly First Class. The article had apparently been forwarded to a mothers' website, which generated about 1,000 e-mails condemning my views; some even wished me a lifetime of sterility. Well, those curses didn't stick, and I was about to introduce my 5-month-old son to the world of air travel. We were catching a quick flight and connecting to another on which his mother would be the pilot.

Upgrade? I couldn't, could I?

It was a temptation, and there was a loophole I could use to get there. After all, I'd never said I wouldn't fly First Class with a baby, just that it shouldn't be allowed. Nevertheless, I turned down the upgrade and took a seat in Economy. At least there was an empty seat next to me.

I had never traveled with an infant before. I normally have a down-pat routine when I fly, but things were different this time. I was now a complete novice, accompanied by a precious bundle of goo. Except for almost putting him through the X-ray machine at security, and leaving him at the airport Starbucks sleeping away in his car seat, things started out relatively well. I had packed like a champ, researched all the different scenarios, and was planning to use this trip as research for a column.

The first thing my boy did upon entering the airplane was to issue the all-knowing grunt that signals a smelly present down under. I rushed to the lavatory before the rest of the passengers boarded, changed his diaper in record time, and returned to my seat. Here I was greeted by many scowls and much rolling of eyes. It was if they were saying, "Oh great, a screaming baby next to us." Oh sure, they were smiling, but you could tell they were secretly looking for an empty seat many rows away. I didn't blame them. I had been in their very position many times before, and I had felt the same way.

I reached into my bag, pulled out a sack full of earplugs, and passed them around to my immediate neighbors. "This is my first trip with my baby, so I don't know if you are going to need these or not," I told them. "But they can't hurt." Not a single person turned me down. We got settled in the seat and prepared for my son's first big trip—well the second, if you count his journey into the world five months earlier.

I had researched baby air travel carefully, and soon had some experience of my own. Here are the eight tips that helped me the most:

1. **Sit carefully.** Many parents of infants favor the bulkhead row because it can accommodate a bassinet. The second-best place is near any engine. The hum of the engine will work like audio Ambien. Even if you don't like the sound of it, you are more apt to sleep if your baby does.

2. **Zip it up.** Bring lots of large zippable plastic bags. They are good for food, but most of all they are good for baby blowout. I was tempted to throw away many items that couldn't be washed up on the airplane, but saved them by zipping them up instead.

3. **Feeding time.** Plan for your baby to eat upon take-off and during the descent for landing. It will relieve the discomfort of changing air pressure in the ears and will distract the baby from strange noises or turbulence.

4. **Packing list.** Never depend on your airline to have any baby amenities. I haven't seen an onboard diaper for years. The following are just a few of the items that proved helpful to me: toys with a tether, a diaper for every hour we were gone, extra outfits for both baby and me, a big travel pack of wet wipes, hand sanitizer, baby Tylenol, and infant gas relief medication.

5. **Proof of age required.** No, not yours, the baby's. Babies under age two fly free if they are held in someone's lap instead of occupying a seat of their own. The person holding the baby must be at least 16 years old. Recently, airlines started cracking down on the two-year-old baby that looks to be more like four, demanding a birth certificate or passport to verify age.

6. **Get some space.** If you are taking an extremely long flight, or you are shepherding older children as well, it might behoove you to buy an extra seat for the baby. Many airlines have infant fares available, and the extra money you spend could save your sanity. As a flight attendant, I've talked to many parents with lap-held children, and the universal comment after a sold-out, nine-hour flight is, "Never again."

7. **Safety first.** Pay for a seat and bring your FAA-approved car seat. Holding a baby during a flight never set well with me before and scares me now that I am a parent. Be sure to pay fresh attention to the safety briefing, for you are handling precious cargo and want to be prepared for all circumstances. If the flight attendant does not bring you an infant life vest before take-off, ask for one. Do not, and I repeat, do not, buckle the seat belt over both you and

the child. If the pilot hits the brakes for any reason, your weight could crush the baby.

8. **Courtesy is a two-way street.** If your baby cries and cries, get up and go to the back of the airplane and try to calm him down. If you are unsuccessful, at least you tried. People will be annoyed—true—but they'll get over it. They were once babies, too, and some of them still are. Note to more understanding passengers: If you see a parent in distress, offer a hand and cut the poor soul some slack.

My first flight was a small nightmare. I think my son sensed my apprehension. He cried, he went through three diapers and one set of clothes (his and mine), and he never quite got settled. When I met up with my wife, I told her I could have used that cocktail in First Class. But something miraculous happened on the next three flights we took, because my boy was a perfect angel. He behaved like a regular frequent flier, and never once complained about the meal service.

My wife made the obligatory embarrassing announcement from the cockpit about her precious onboard cargo, made a perfect landing, and sat beaming as many cockpit photos were taken. It was a successful trip, and I had managed it without giving in to the First Class temptation. But I will be honest with you, if they had offered me the First Class seat or nothing, I would have taken it in a second, and I probably would have enjoyed that cocktail, as well.

10 Embarassing Flight Moments

One of my favorite ways to get to know fellow crewmembers is to ask, "What is your most embarrassing moment on a flight or a layover?" It's a great way to pass the time, and some of my best stories come from their responses.

Usually, people respond cautiously with "I don't know—what's yours?"

I tell them about the time I inhaled a piece of chicken in the back galley as I was confronted by my airline's CEO, and then proceeded to choke and cough it back up on his shoes.

Or how, on a layover in downtown New York, I got out of the shower, dancing and singing to one of my favorite rock songs. I stopped short in front of a window, where I found myself two feet away from an office building with no fewer than eight people laughing and clapping. Not only was I naked, but my dancing is nothing short of horrifying and should not be viewed by anyone under any circumstances.

After breaking the ice with this vivid image, wild stories are sure to follow.

Enjoy these top 10 embarrassing stories that I have heard:

1. An older flight attendant serving meals was down to her last lasagna. As she passed it to a passenger, her top denture popped out of her mouth and landed directly in the middle of the pasta. She froze in embarrassment. The passenger calmly and discreetly said, "That's OK, I'll take the beef instead."

2. A pilot with a multi-segment flight ahead of him had to declare his inability to continue after the first flight. He had a bad case of gas, and his captain refused to work with him. The airline had to cancel the next two segments. Months later, a review board took up the case of the canceled flights, and the poor pilot had to explain to a committee about his intestinal fortitude. He laughs about it now, but nobody was then amused by his quip: "I can proudly say we had plenty of gas."

3. A young female flight attendant happened to have her fiance onboard. When he went to use the lavatory, she thought it would be a fun joke to unlock the door and join him. Well, she unlocked the wrong restroom and surprised a first-class passenger doing his business.

4. During breakfast service on a flight to London, while most passengers slumbered away, a flight attendant accidentally hooked a man's toupee with her ring. Not knowing what the dark, furry things was, she started screaming, thus waking a shocked group of passengers and one very embarrassed man.

5. During the safety demonstration, someone, (no, not me) slipped a live air (CO_2) cartridge into a young flight attendant's safety vest. When she pulled down on the cord to inflate the vest, she got a loud noise and full inflation. This scared the young lady so much that she began crying and wet her pants.

6. On a layover, a female flight attendant, who had had too much to drink, walked into an unlocked room, thinking it was her own, undressed and climbed into bed. Minutes later, she started screaming as the room's rightful occupant (a male) walked out of the bathroom naked. It took more than an hour to clear up the situation.

7. Another flight attendant liked to make love in odd places. On a layover, she took her boyfriend up to the hotel roof for a little fun. What they didn't know was that the blacked-out glass of the adjoining room was really a one-way window and that a conference was taking place inside. Let's just say that everyone had a good seat.

8. A captain, his girlfriend, who was a flight attendant, and the co-pilot, their good friend, were all working the same flight. The two pilots decided to play a joke on the girlfriend by undressing mid flight. They called the girlfriend to come up to the cockpit, but she had been called to the back at the last minute. An older flight attendant with no sense of humor answered the call instead. She reported what she saw and both pilots got fired. How do you explain that on your résumé?

9. At the end of a flight, a young flight attendant, who was shy, managed to walk out of the lavatory, through the airport, and up to her hotel room with her entire skirt tucked into her panty hose. Considering it was LAX, she was sure to have put on a show for quite a few people.

10. On her way to a layover and her best friend's bachelorette party, a flight attendant was stopped by a security guard, who had heard a strange humming coming from her suitcase. A search of the bag turned up the party favors: three vibrators (one of them activated), handcuffs, and an inflatable man.

Given the proper stimulus, most every crewmember can give me an embarrassing story. But not one flight attendant, who flew with me one time into San Francisco. She claimed to be boring and had no story to tell. Well, during the layover, at about 2 o' clock in the morning, there was a frantic knock on my door. When I opened the door, she was standing there in her panties with an arm covering her naked chest. I quickly told her that she had misunderstood the situation and that I was married. She stormed through my door, picked up the phone, and asked the front desk for a room key to be sent up. She apparently had gotten up to use the bathroom and in a sleepy stupor went through the hall door instead.

I guess that was an embarrassing moment for both of us.

Lost and Found

How many times have you lost something on-board an airplane? Did it get swallowed by a hungry seat pocket in front of you, or did it fall under your seat?

If someone finds it, where does it go and do you have a chance to get it back?

The answer depends on two things: what you misplaced and when you discovered the loss.

If you realize you're missing something within minutes of deplaning, run back to the gate and ask an agent to escort you down to the plane. If the cleaners haven't finished, then the odds are in your favor. As a rule, the earlier the discovery, the better your chances for recovery.

The airlines have a lost-and-found center, usually located by the baggage claim area. But you have to understand that many airplanes have minimal airport stays and are quickly turned around for maximum efficiency. That means the cleaners are rushed through their duties, do a sub-standard job, and miss many items. So your item may have been lost in New York but could end up in a California lost-and-found center.

If it is a book you lost, then forget about it. Many passengers leave their books onboard on purpose, intended for someone else who hasn't read it. I actually collect books I find after flights. I have over 2,500 of them sitting in my library waiting until my retirement to be read. I have something on every topic from Buddhism to *The Joy of Sex*; I just hope I am able to enjoy the latter when I retire.

If it is a valuable item, then it has to get by the cleaners, flight attendants, gate agents, and finally, the lost-and-found agent.

I would like to believe in universal honesty but it's not always practiced. Once I went to the lost-and-found office and told them I lost my iPod. The agent chuckled, "I haven't seen one of those here in months. You can probably write that off as gone for good." I noticed a pair of iPod headphones hanging out of his coat jacket, which was only a coincidence, I'm sure.

In the lost-and-found, I have discovered a wide range of items, such as cell phones, eyeglasses, coats, baby toys, shoes, and even some gadgets resembling marital aids, but I didn't investigate those too closely.

The biggest surprise was the box full of dentures that passengers had undoubtedly left on meal trays. I spent over an hour in the office poking around and taking notes. It was like a dysfunctional Christmas, full of items about which you wondered why, what, how, and where.

What about purses and wallets? If you are like me when it comes to losing your wallet, the money is the least of your worries. I don't care if the money is gone, just as long as I get back the rest—credit cards, licenses, photos, and contact cards. Wallets and purses have a good chance of being returned because they usually carry identification, so don't give in to despair too quickly.

One day a Hispanic aircraft cleaner approached me and handed me a wallet she had found. Her English was broken but she kept repeating,

"Mucho money inside." I opened it and counted about $2,500. I turned it over to the gate agent and told her where and who found it.

A man eventually claimed it, hardly batting an eye. He didn't even check the contents.

I think there is a lot of goodness in this world when someone who works 12-hour shifts for minimum wage doesn't even consider slipping the money into her pocket.

The man probably should have left a tip for her but didn't, so I gave the young lady a twenty dollar bill in appreciation for her honesty, which renewed my hope in mankind, and the guilty thoughts that had crossed my mind of keeping the money for myself.

That reminds me of a joke on the same subject:

> Virgin Airways is hiring flight attendants but only has one job available for the last three female applicants. They will be asked one question, and then a choice will be made based on their answer. The question is: "If you found a wallet on the airplane what would you do?"
>
> The first applicant answers, "I would return the wallet and all of its contents to the rightful owner."
>
> The second applicant answers, "I would return the wallet but keep the money."
>
> The third one answers, "I would keep the money and throw away everything else."
>
> So which one did they hire?
>
> The one with the blonde hair and big chest.

Sorry, but a crewmember from Virgin told me that one.

Flying With Fluffy

When you are on a flight you expect to hear an occasional crying baby, the engines whooshing, a flight attendant shouting about the seat belt sign. But a bark, meow—or even a cock-a-doodle-doo? Not really.

The Air Transport Association estimates that more than a half a million dogs and cats are transported on commercial airlines each year, and 99 percent reach their destinations without incident. Which is great, but it's small consolation if your pet was part of that remaining one percent.

Besides the usual dog or cat in-flight, I have flown with lizards, snakes, fish, chickens, pigs, monkeys, ferrets, a fox, several birds, and even a rat (although he was a stowaway).

I remember a few times when the animals have either escaped from their cages, had bouts of explosive diarrhea, or were involved in on-board pet fights.

The most memorable was a parrot named Fluffy. Because she was great at repeating phrases, we allowed the owner to take her out of the carrier and let her hang out in the back galley with the flight attendants.

We taught Fluffy how to repeat all the flight attendant sayings like "chicken or beef," "seat belt sign is on," and "coffee, tea or me."

If a passenger came back and asked for two or more drinks, Fluffy would let out our favorite phrase of "high-maintenance flier," which had all of us in hysterics. We stationed Fluffy at the door after we landed and as people deplaned, she squawked "buh-bye" to every passenger.

Many people consider their pets as important family members. I know, because I have five cats and sometimes wonder where I fit in my wife's pecking order.

There are many do's and don'ts out there when it comes to traveling with pets. The following is a list I have compiled for a better pet flight experience:

1. Never sedate your pet without the explicit permission of your vet. High altitudes and sedatives are usually a dangerous combination. While many of us choose to anesthetize ourselves in-flight, it's not a good idea for your animal.

2. Contact your airline before flying with your pet. Write down all of your questions ahead of time, and remember that there are no stupid questions. Okay, maybe you can leave out the one about pet parachutes.

3. The carry-on option is by far the best if your animal is small enough. You have to book early though, as there are limits on the number of pets allowed in the cabin at one time.

4. If it is possible, book a non-stop flight or at least one with minimal time layovers between flights. Most animal fatalities take place on the ground.

5. Make sure your pet has some type of identification collar or tag with all necessary details, since there have been times when pets have escaped from their kennel. Bring a leash for walking and a scooper just in case.

6. Check all conditions regarding flight and health. If there is supposed to be a heat wave or a blizzard where you are going, then put it off for a couple of weeks. Same goes for your pet's health; if it is ill, then delay. Better safe than sorry.

7. Choose a carrier designed for air travel and familiarize your pet with it well ahead of time. Consider length, width, and height.

8. Don't feed your pet too much before a flight, for obvious reasons. You may think that guy with foot rot is cabin enemy number one, but just wait till your precious Fifi clears her intestines and creates a smelly morsel half her size. Instead, get a calorie supplement from your local pet store or vet.

9. If your pet is too big to bring onboard, have some compassion. Your pet has to go into a dark scary place filled with weird noises and unfamiliar motion. Lessen the trauma by adding his favorite blanket and a chew toy or two.

10. Ask about getting frequent flier points. I am serious, because many people don't know that if you have to pay extra for your pet, most airlines will accept them as bona fide frequent flier club members.

11. Most of all, ask your veterinarian for any special instructions.

There is a new FAA travel regulation that gives passengers the right to bring along any animal. Yes, if a doctor approves an application stating that an animal provides a certain level of emotional comfort, the airline is required, by law, to provide transportation. This was the case of the in-flight pig that caused a ruckus not so long ago, and the Shetland pony who is now a frequent flier on SkyWest.

There is a flight attendant I know who has a second job transporting pets. The money is secondary as she has a real passion for animals and would rather see a reunited pet as opposed to a newly inducted member of the animal shelter.

What was her most embarrassing moment? A snake that got out of its carrier in-flight and was spotted slithering down the toilet. This was after the blood-curdling screams from a rather large half-dressed woman who came rushing out of the lav.

Luckily, for the pet courier, the snake was recovered alive, albeit blue and smelly, during the emptying of the septic tanks.

There is a well known story in the airline industry about a bizarre pet occurrence. One day as the baggage workers were offloading bags from a flight, they discovered a dog kennel containing a dead golden lab puppy.

They felt awful about it and noticed that it was connecting on a flight more than three hours away. A couple of the men went out on their lunch break, adopted a new puppy and substituted it for the dead one. Their hope was that some small boy waiting for his beloved pet would not notice the switch and be happy at their reunion.

At the final destination, great cheers rang out, along with "It's a miracle, it's a miracle." The family of the golden lab was convinced of a higher being's intervention.

Apparently, the puppy had died during their vacation, and they were merely transporting it home to be buried.

An investigation quickly followed. This was mainly to prevent the misconception that transporting dead animals at 40,000 feet might bring them back to life.

The responsible workers were at first given two weeks suspension with pay, but which quickly became a "Reward for Honorable Service," after the airline received a great deal of positive press for their deed.

Turbulent Times

The inspiration for this chapter comes from a close call. My own flight was uneventful, but the airplane I was about to board, which had just flown in from the Caribbean, had experienced severe air turbulence. So severe, in fact, that five passengers and all three flight attendants had to be taken to the hospital upon arrival.

It was a close call for me as I had been scheduled to be one of those flight attendants, but had traded for another flight. The first thing I noticed was that the paint around the wings was chipped off in a perfect circle. I can't say for sure that the damage was caused by this episode of turbulence, but the airplane had been freshly painted.

Our departure was delayed because the airplane needed extensive onboard cleaning. Apparently, several passengers had lost control of their bodily functions. In fact, the cleaners were doing something I had never seen before: They were cleaning the ceiling. The ceiling stains included red wine, coffee, and vomit, and I am almost positive I saw lipstick. The mechanic came aboard to announce he had run the necessary airplane stress tests and that everything had checked out A-OK. I was glad to hear it, but I wondered how the person who owned those lips was doing.

Apparently, the captain had put on the seat belt sign because of reports of choppy air ahead. One moment the three flight attendants were in the aisle checking that seat belts were fastened, and the next moment they hit the ceiling—along with five other passengers who had failed to buckle up. When we boarded the passengers for the next flight, you could tell which ones had been aboard during the turbulence. They were the ones with the scared expressions still branded on their faces. One female passenger broke out in tears with her first step through the doorway. That must have been one bad flight.

Turbulence can be described as an unseen stream of air in irregular motion; it often occurs unexpectedly. Several conditions give rise to turbulence. The most common is flying in the vicinity of a thunderstorm. Others include flying through clouds, flying over mountainous areas with a prevailing wind, flying near high-altitude jet streams, flying in a frontal system, and flying in an air mass that is experiencing extreme temperature changes.

Here are 10 things you might not have known about turbulence:

1. All turbulence results from the collision of air masses moving at different speeds.

2. Turbulence falls into three categories: light, medium, and severe. Light turbulence can be compared to traveling along a bumpy road. Medium turbulence is more like four-wheeling over rough terrain. Severe turbulence is like riding a roller coaster, only not as much fun.

3. "CAT," or clear air turbulence, occurs when the sky is clear of clouds. It usually occurs when flying from a slow-moving air mass into or near a jet stream moving at high speed.

4. "Wake turbulence" is created by other airplanes. Some of the airflow slides down the wing and spirals off the wingtips creating small horizontal tornados. While it does not last long, this wake turbulence can play havoc with an unsuspecting aircraft that flies through it before it has dissipated.

5. You are more likely to get turbulence over land than over the ocean. The most severe turbulence occurs when flying north to south (or vice versa) rather than east to west. In my experience, the worst turbulence often occurs over the equator.

6. Turbulence occurs more often in winter than summer due to more frontal systems and their accompanying strong winds.

7. The term "air pocket," an erroneous description of air turbulence, was coined by a journalist during World War I. The term has caused needless worry to passengers who believe that an airplane could drop a few hundred feet if it flew through one. Although it may seem like a drop of hundreds or even thousands of feet, in reality the airplane seldom drops more than 20 or 30 feet. It seems far because the airplane drops very suddenly.

8. "Wind shear" describes a rapid change in wind direction over a very short distance. It is most risky to aircraft during takeoff and landing, when the plane is close to the ground and has little time or altitude to recover. Although all turbulence creates wind shear, the term is most often used in conjunction with turbulent air that is associated with thunderstorms and occurs near the ground.

9. The wings of a commercial aircraft have practically no chance of being torn off by turbulence. In fact, it is the flexibility of the wings that gives the airplane its resilience. If the wings were rigid, they would surely snap. I once watched a wing bounce all over the place during a terrible bout of turbulence, but after seeing a documentary on the making of the 777 and the stress tests all airplanes undergo, I never give the wings a second thought.

10. In-flight turbulence is the leading cause of injury to airline passengers and flight attendants. Each year, about 60 air passengers in the United States are injured by turbulence while not wearing their seat belts.

I have just one tip for you about air turbulence and I'm sure you can guess what it is. Yes: Fasten that seat belt and pay attention to the seat belt signs. Few passengers have been seriously hurt during air turbulence when they were wearing their seat belts.

Once on a flight, an extremely obnoxious frequent flyer explained to me and everyone around him that under no circumstances was he to be disturbed. He then put on his eye mask and went to sleep. During the flight, when we encountered severe air turbulence, the passenger awoke three feet in the air. He hurt his tailbone on the armrest as he dropped to his seat. Later the man tried to sue the airline for not properly warning him to fasten his seat belt. Unluckily for him, his "Do not disturb" instruction had been heard by just about every passenger onboard. It's the one time I can say that an obnoxious passenger literally became a pain in the ass.

Buckle up!

PC Tips for Your PC

I t's your notebook, workmate, business consultant, mobile office, movie theater, and—more often than not—your solitaire buddy.

The variety of traveling PCs is mind-boggling: from widescreen to compact to tablet to palm-size. Whichever the kind you have, your PC is often a hassle when you fly. You search for power to feed it, you tote around endless accessories, you juggle it at security, and you look for places to stash it on-board.

Come to think of it, it's a lot like a baby—but that's another story.

As a flight attendant, I've seen my share of PC woes. Here are 10 tips to make your computer a better travel companion:

1. **Power up.** If you think you'll be able to juice up between flights, think again. Outlets for passenger use are disappearing as fast as

airport energy bills are rising, and when you do find an outlet, it usually has someone hooked up to it already. So bring an extra battery—it's worth the weight.

2. **Choose your seat wisely.** On the airplane, get a seat by the window so you are not bothered by passengers with weak bladders. If possible, get a seat in an exit row, at the front of the economy section, or on the bulkhead aisle; these rows typically have more space—or have no seats in front of them—so you can extend your screen without interference.

3. **Protect against snoopers.** If you have WiFi access on your computer, secure it. When I turn on my computer in-flight, I often find I can access most of the laptops on-board. So, if you don't want me—or any other nosy person—looking into your files, learn how to secure your connection.

4. **Cover your ears.** If you (or your child) want to play a game or watch a movie, be considerate and wear earplugs. If someone in a neighboring row is not using earplugs, and the audio annoys you, call the flight attendant. Common courtesy will work through most problems.

5. **Close it up.** When flight attendants pass with the drink cart, close your screen until they have served everyone in your row. Accidents and turbulence can cause spillage onto your keyboard, ruining your flight and possibly your PC.

6. **Get your Net for free.** Many airports offer free wireless Internet access these days, but not all of them. If you have WiFi capability on your laptop, go to <u>freewifispot.com</u> to find out where you can access the Internet for free.

7. **Extend it.** Check with your airline to see if your flight has an in-seat power supply. If it does, then spend 10 or 12 bucks on a universal flight adapter cable. Different computers have different power cords, so check the specifications carefully; some models come with different plugs so they can adapt to most any laptop—as well to cell phones, PDAs, and DVD players.

8. **Eyes front!** Why is it that when your computer is open, everyone feels it's OK to look at your business? I have to admit I am guilty of this impropriety myself from time to time. If you really must keep your work to yourself, invest in a privacy filter to keep prying eyes off. 3M and other manufacturers make several models.

9. **Be considerate of others.** Porn and flying don't mix. I had to stop four passengers last year from playing X-rated DVDs. Why anyone would want to be turned on during a flight is beyond me. Different strokes for different folks—just not on the airplane!

10. **Back it up.** Technically, you are not allowed to put your laptop in the seat pocket in front of you for takeoff or landing, but did you know it's OK to put it behind your back against the seat? This is actually a good idea: The computer poses no danger to anyone and there is no way you'll leave it behind accidentally.

Laptops are an ingrained way of life for most of us now, and as technology expands, so too will the services and places that support them. For instance, in the works are power stations at airports where you can quick-charge a dying battery, and you will soon find free WiFi spots in most airports, as well as DVD-rental stands in many terminals.

Technology is fascinating as well as frustrating, and the airline that keeps up with current technological requirements will win out in the end.

What a Steal!

With all the other worries associated with air travel—terrorism, airline bankruptcy, long lines at security—few people worry about theft. No, I don't mean the ticket price or the price of coffee at the airport. I don't even mean those airline CEOs getting away with robbery every time they cash their paychecks. No, the thief I mean is the one sitting next to you on the airplane.

In my 18 years in the airline business, I have dealt with stolen bags, laptops, cameras, and purses. I have seen pickpockets in action, and I've seen thieves slip jewelry off fellow travelers while they were sleeping. What I've learned is that travel is a stressful time for most people, and there are other people out there who are happy to take advantage of your inattention.

Here's what you can do to minimize the risk of theft when you fly:

1. **Hang it up carefully.** If you are in the habit of hanging your jacket or coat in the closet, take all your valuables—especially your wallet—out of the pockets. That's the first place a thief will look.

2. **Mark your bags.** More and more bags look alike these days, so put something on your luggage that makes it stand out from the rest: a sticker or ribbon—anything that makes a mix-up impossible. This will prevent the intentional—and unintentional—misappropriation of your property.

3. **Dummy up.** Carry a "dummy" wallet or purse that contains only one credit card, $20 in cash and one form of identification. Put the rest of the usual contents in your carry-on bag. That way, you'll have less to lose if the dummy is lifted or lost.

4. **Walk it through.** If there is a long security line, your bags may clear the X-ray screener before you make it through the metal detector. Wait until you are ready to walk through the machine before releasing your purse, wallet, or laptop. Sure, there is camera surveillance at security, but your thief will be long gone before any review takes place. Fact: More items go missing in the security line than from any other place.

5. **Stow it nearby.** Once you're on the airplane, keep your carry-on bag nearby. Some back-of-the-plane passengers think it's smart to stow their bag up front, for an easy grab during deplaning. Believe me, a watchful thief can grab that bag a lot faster than you can push and shove your way to the front of the line.

6. **Bury the treasure.** If you put your billfold or any other valuables in your bag, don't put them in the outermost compartments. That's pretty much telling a thief, "Help yourself."

7. **Watch your seat.** Be careful when storing your bag under the seat in front of you; don't face any pockets forward, or the passenger in front of you may walk off with your goods. Also, never leave anything of value on your seat when you leave it to go to the lavatory or to take a stroll.

8. **Do not pass go.** Take special care of your passport and know where it is at all times. Losing your passport will ruin your entire trip; trust me on this one.

9. **Exercise common sense.** Carry your purse with the opening facing toward you, and keep your wallet out of your back pocket. I know this sounds obvious, but when people go flying, common sense often gets checked with the baggage.

10. **Speak up.** Don't overreact if you catch someone handling your bag (innocent mistakes do happen), but be firm nonetheless. Similarly, if you witness a theft, tell someone immediately—a flight attendant, gate agent, security guard—anyone. I'm sure you would want their help if you were the victim.

I once knew a flight attendant who had a second job as a "naughty party" planner. On her way to a convention, another passenger made off with her bags. She frantically searched the airplane after everyone had deplaned and even ran out into the terminal to see if she could spot her bags, but they were long gone. The worst part of the ordeal was having to provide a detailed description of each bag's contents, she said.

But can you imagine the face of the person who opened the luggage? Whether it was theft or confusion, someone got the surprise of a lifetime!

The Dreaded Red-Eye

Ah, the "red-eye." If it were such a great experience, don't you think they would call it the "bright-eyed and bushy-tailed"? Well, they don't, and there's a reason for it: These all-night flights can be miserable.

In my humble opinion, human beings were never intended to sleep sitting up. Whenever I take a red-eye flight, my tailbone ends up hurting and my neck gets sore from the Dozing Head Bob. Of course, there's little chance of sleep anyway. During the flight, announcements will be made, babies will cry and Murphy's Law decrees that every cabin will have at least one hefty gentleman who has perfected the art of snoring.

If you do nod off, it will be just moments before the flight attendant turns on the overhead lights to prepare the airplane for landing.

This is always a moment of keen embarrassment, because in the glare of the light you suddenly know with absolute certainty that you look just as bedraggled as everyone around you. To make matters worse, you probably have "death breath," which you got from that small bag of barbequed cardboard sticks they handed out with the drinks four hours ago.

Bleary-eyed and sleep-deprived, you emerge from the aircraft crumpled and smelly. You have jet lag and you're in a bad mood. No, I don't think there is a "full day's work" anywhere in your immediate future.

This is probably not the experience you had in mind when you booked your ticket (though, come to think of it, it is the same experience you had the last time you flew the red-eye). Does it always have to be like this? Not really. I've been working as a flight attendant for 17 years, and I've thought a lot about it. Here are my top 10 tips for a better late-night flight:

1. **Go before you go.** Wait until you are about to board and then use the restroom in the airport. Even if you think you don't have to go, go anyway. The restroom is roomier and cleaner than the lavatory on the airplane, and there's nothing worse than falling asleep on the red-eye only to wake up 15 minutes later with the urge. Odds are that when you return to your seat, sleep won't.

2. **Practice hydration moderation.** It is always good to drink water before, during, and after a flight, but don't overdo it on a red-eye or you'll be running to the lavatory every five seconds. Nothing says you can't drink water toward the end or after your flight.

3. **Plug it up.** I have said it before and will keep on saying it: Bring your earplugs. Tuning out the announcements, babies, excessive talkers, and especially the hefty snorers is a must for deep sleep.

4. **Wear a mask.** Bring a comfortable eye mask with you. It will keep you from being distracted during the flight, and when the flight attendant turns the bright lights on, you won't feel like committing air rage.

5. **Cushion the blow.** Travel shops sell a small, blow-up cushion that fits under your posterior and comforts your tailbone. It looks like a whoopee cushion and it works likes a charm for me.

6. **Position yourself.** On a red-eye, the best seat is a window seat (unless you have a bladder problem, of course). You don't have to worry about your seatmate waking you every time he gets up, and the window doubles as a headrest. Get to the airport early and request a window seat as soon as possible.

7. **Do the can-can.** When the flight attendant comes around for drink requests, ask for an unopened can of something you want to drink later. This way when you wake up wanting a drink in the middle of the flight, you can quench your thirst and go right back to sleep.

8. **Be a pill.** I can't and don't recommend taking heavy prescription sleep medications when you fly, but there are over-the-counter sleep aids that might help enough to make the difference.

9. **Brace yourself.** Stop the Dozing Head Bob with one of those horseshoe-shaped neck pillows. (Have you ever watched someone bobbing for hours? It looks pretty moronic, doesn't it? Well, this is exactly how you look, too.) I've thrown my neck out one too many times to fly an all-nighter without one. If you think you'll be given a pillow on-board, think again. Airlines are tightening their belts, and pillows have become scarce.

10. **Conquer death breath.** There is nothing worse than yawning and almost passing out from your own breath, so put some powerful mints or a breath freshener in your pocket. Offer some to your seat neighbors, too.

You have to do what you have to do, and you have to fly when you must. You may say, "Never again!" after a red-eye flight, but chances are, you'll be back. Just come a little better prepared next time, and think of me when you're blinded by the overhead lights in the morning.

Jet Lag Tips From the Crew

I f you travel enough, sooner or later you will fall victim to the ever-popular traveling syndrome unofficially known as "hyperboeing-tinnitus," "the funk," or more commonly known as jet lag. It is the feeling of severe lack of energy, weird sleeping patterns, always being tired, no vigor, depression and about a day or two of being in a daze. As far as I know, nobody has ever died from jet lag, but sometimes you feel as if you are dead inside. Jet lag occurs when a traveler passes over a number of time zones that disrupt the normal circadian rhythm which helps humans wake up in the morning and go to sleep at night. Some say it's caused by dehydration from the airplane trip, altitude sickness, lack of sleep, and even from polar radiation. While all of these may be true, the one definite factor is the change in sleeping patterns. You arrive in Italy and it may be 1 o'clock in the afternoon, but your body is not convinced, insisting that it is 3 in the morning.

Other factors include the stale cabin air, dry atmosphere, lack of exercise or movement, your current health, and the worrying and anticipation of the trip. While traveling may be a wondrous occasion, it can be quite a stressful one as well. Some prepare too much, while others not enough. Some people drink too much on the flight (I am more inclined to say that is a hangover instead of jet lag). All of these are contributing factors to this syndrome.

Jet lag tends to be more severe traveling from west to east as you are losing time, while east to west is less severe because you are gaining time and more apt to transition into your normal daily activities easier.

A commonly asked question is whether or not crewmembers get jet lag. There is no simple answer. Some do and some don't. The ones that usually don't are the ones that fly similar trips with similar hours. Say I have a month of trips, flying to South America, to Asia, to Germany, and the last one being a shuttle trip across America. I pretty much accept the fact that I am going to be in a deep jet lag for most of the month. However, if I were to fly to London every week at the same time, my jet lag would be minimal.

Speaking for myself, most of the time I don't get jet lag. It's all in the sleep pattern. I can stay awake for 36 hours straight and then sleep for 20 plus at a time. It is only when I don't disrupt my sleeping pattern that my jet lag sets in. For example, if I have two weeks off and I don't fly anywhere, my sleep pattern returns to what people consider normal. This seems to disturb my pattern of disrupted sleep. I know it is fairly hard to comprehend, but it isn't if you live it.

Here is a list of some crewmember preventive jet lag measures. While many of these tips seem like common sense, often we seem to check that in along with our luggage.

1. **Try to get some sleep on the plane.** You'd be surprised how many people force themselves to stay awake for the movie. Bring earplugs, a neck pillow, and eyeshades—anything to help you get some sleep.

2. **Don't overdo the stimulants.** Limit the booze, coffee, and sleeping pills. They may do for an immediate fix, but might affect you negatively.

3. **Water with a twist.** Try to hydrate (water) yourself more than the flight dehydrates you. One of the best tips that seem to work well for me is the water supplement method. Instead of drinking plain water, add some type of juice (I recommend cranberry); this way instead of flushing your system, you retain more. Comparing my jet lag symptoms after drinking plain water versus adding juice, I have always felt better with the combo.

4. **Take supplemental vitamins before, during, and after your trip.** Also, a skin moisturizer is a good item to have nearby at all times. Melatonin and zinc have had reportedly good results for jet lag. Eat lots of vegetables and healthy foods, or at least bring some supplemental bran with you.

5. **Take a long hot shower as frequently as you can.** You may feel paralytic when you first wake up but get into the shower and feel 100% better immediately. If you are up to it, go for a long walk or a run when you settle in. The more oxygen, fresh air, and exercise, the better.

6. **Stay away from products claiming to be miracle jet-lag cures.** I have seen everything from lights under the knee-caps to polar radiation hats. The only thing these items will reduce is your wallet size.

7. **When you arrive, try to adapt to the new time of day immediately.** For example, force yourself to stay awake until the time of day you would normally go to sleep back home. Don't try to see everything in one day. That is, of course, as long as you have more than one day.

8. **Get up and stretch.** Okay, maybe not during the flight, but your body is not used to sitting down or sleeping in an upright position. Break it up a bit, instead of ringing your call button, come get a drink in the back. We don't bite . . . well, most of us don't.

9. **If you are returning from a holiday, or a long business trip, allow a couple of days afterwards to recover.** Don't go into work the next day.

10. **Don't worry so much.** Try to have fun—even if you are on business or if the trip is costing you a fortune. Life is an adventure, and this is just another chapter of it.

There was a finding by a Swedish scientist that proved that sexual intimacy the night before a flight lessened the symptoms of jet lag. I anxiously showed a copy of the article to my wife, and she replied that I had better find a new job. Not exactly the result what I was hoping for. Good luck and may you be jet lag free.

Tips for the Long Haul

S ure, you've been on short flights, medium flights, and maybe even some pretty long flights—say, eight or 10 hours. But have you ever taken a super long-haul flight, spending 12 or 16 hours in the air? I recently did. In fact, I jumped at the chance to fly direct from New York to Tokyo.

I didn't give the 15-hour flight time much thought. That is, not until the day of departure, when I did the math. Fifteen hours? That is equivalent to 900 minutes, nine movies, six football games and two well-rested nights of sleep in a row. Maybe I was being unduly pessimistic, but any way I looked at it, it spelled l-o-n-g.

Can an airplane fly that long without a fuel stop? Could favorable winds speed up the flight? Would I go stir-crazy? All very good questions. I would soon find out the answers.

The plane was tugged out to the runway in order not to waste any precious fuel. The age and demeanor of the flight crew seemed different from what you get on a one-hour flight. The flight attendants were more senior, quite a bit less perky, and they looked to be pacing themselves for the journey ahead. On take-off, the airplane, weighted down with passengers, cargo, and fuel, struggled to get airborne.

I had dinner, a drink, a movie, and a short nap. When I awoke, I figured the flight had to be at least half over. Piece of cake, I chuckled to myself. Then I looked at the air map and read the fatal line: "Time Left Until Arrival: 12.06 hours." I slouched back in my seat and tried to regroup.

This was going to be tougher than I thought. I penned idle thoughts to pass the time. Here are some of them.

You know you've been on an airplane too long when:

- Your rear end is numb and has taken on the shape of the seat cushion.
- The flight attendants start looking like prison guards.
- The airline food starts tasting great.
- You understand the cockpit announcements perfectly.
- You forget where you're going and no longer care.
- You start looking for the parachutes.

During the flight I also wrote this chapter, hoping to turn my misery into some advice others could use. Here are some tips for the long haul:

1. **Make yourself comfortable.** If you can use your mileage points for an upgrade, this is definitely the time to do it. Similarly, if the airline has a section in the Economy section with roomier seats at a nominal price, pay it. Fifteen hours is a long time to play the cheapskate.

2. **Don't be a clock watcher.** If you can refrain from constantly looking at the air map and the "Time Until Arrival" page, you will save your sanity.

3. **Delay the z's.** Watch the movie, have a drink, eat a meal, read a book, do something to keep you awake as long as possible. When you finally do get some sleep, it will be heavier and longer, and when you awake, you should have the better part of the flight behind you.

4. **Turn a deaf ear.** I have said it before and will keep on saying it: Bring your earplugs. Tuning out announcements, babies, excessive talkers, and especially the hefty snorers is critical for deep sleep.

5. **Circulate.** Get up, stretch and walk around as often as you can. Deep-vein thrombosis—the formation of blood clots in deep veins of the lower legs—can be a serious risk on these flights.

6. **Keep busy.** Bring books, puzzles, gadgets—anything to occupy your time. If you are bringing a laptop, be sure to include an extra battery, especially if you plan to watch DVDs.

7. **Get a window on the world.** Unless you have a bladder problem, the best place to sit is at a window seat. You won't have to worry about your seatmates waking you every time they have to use the lavatory, and you can use the window for a head rest. Get to the airport early and request a window seat at check-in.

8. **Go back.** If you get hungry during the flight, head to the back of the airplane. Many times the flight attendants have set up a snack cart in the galley for people who get hungry or just want to graze.

9. **Dress down.** It is not unusual for passengers on long-haul flights to change into pajamas. In fact, I spied two First Class passengers handing their pants to the flight attendants to hang up. But anything comfortable will do, so long as it won't wrinkle into a ball in the course of the flight. But be sure to wear your lace-up shoes, not slippers. Your feet tend to swell on long flights, and they may not fit back into your shoes at the end of the flight. This has happened to me three times.

10. **Feed the bear.** A long flight is no time to start a diet. Sometimes a candy bar or two can take the edge off and keep you from becoming a grumbling mess. Similarly, if you are a smoker, bring nicotine gum, as this is not the occasion to try to go cold turkey.

Currently, the longest scheduled commercial flight is from Newark, New Jersey, to Singapore, flown by Singapore Airlines. The flight time is a mind-boggling $18^{1/2}$ hours, but if I had to choose an airline to be stuck on for that long, it would definitely be Singapore Airlines.

I arrived exhausted but was happy to breathe outdoor air once again, even if it was mingled with jet fumes. But then I confronted one of the great mysteries of life: Why is it that, after sitting for 15 hours, you just want to sit down again?

I have certainly developed new respect for the flight crews and businessmen who tackle these flights on a routine basis. I hope when you find yourself on such a flight, you can use some of these tips. Just keep telling yourself: What goes up, must eventually come down.

PART THREE

Airlines and Employees

CHAPTER ONE

Bite Your Tongue

Many poorly-chosen words are uttered by air travelers to flight attendants. And while we've become accustomed to hearing them, it's never easy to be on the receiving end.

Like what?

How about when passengers come up to you and whisper, "I have a bad feeling about this flight," as we're boarding. They haven't seen anything or heard specific threats, but they have a "bad feeling." If you have a bad feeling about a flight, don't spread your doubts to me. I can't go to the captain with, "I think we better cancel because the lady in 21A has a bad feeling about the flight." If I am superstitious, then I will be on edge the entire trip.

"You look tired," is another one. I have never understood why anyone would say this. It is a no-win statement. If the flight attendant wasn't tired, you have just made her feel it, and if she is truly tired you have now made her feel doubly so. At present, with the new contract rules, it is not uncommon for a typical workday to consist of 16 hours or five legs a day.

A passenger in Economy was flirting with an elderly flight attendant, who was somewhat interested until the fatal line of "You must have been a knock-out." Her smile promptly turned into a scowl and the possibility of a future date was gone.

The words "must have been" should stay well away from any pick-up line. Believe it or not, I have heard it said several times, and not once did it go over well. Incidentally, this also qualifies as the worst in-flight pick-up line next to remarks about the "Mile High Club applications."

Here's another one. During boarding a frustrated passenger announces to the flight attendant, "I am never flying this airline again." Now my question is, why would anybody say that, especially at the beginning of a flight? At that moment we are probably thinking, "Good riddance." Plus, if you aren't going to fly on our airline again, we don't really care if you have a good flight or not, and will therefore probably not treat you so royally.

How about this one: Our airline threatens to go into bankruptcy protection and instead of common courtesy or concern for our careers, the passengers ask about the status of their frequent flier points should the airline go under. While I realize that it is a very good question, a little consideration for the future of airline employees would be appreciated. What's even worse is that my friends and family usually ask this as well.

"Smile!" Sounds like a fairly harmless saying, but it is another of those no-win statements. If the flight attendant is in a bad mood then she will be even more so upon hearing this. If she isn't in a bad mood, you have just placed her in one. I fly with an elderly lady who always looks like she is frowning, even when she is actually smiling. She got so fed up with people telling her to smile that she now tells them that her husband died yesterday. It makes those who said it feel incredibly guilty and simultaneously teaches them a lesson.

And how about this one: "When is the baby due?" Three, two, one, kaboom! "I'm not pregnant!" Oops. Now, with the absence of the weight policy, this happens more than you think.

"I wouldn't want your job for anything!" At that point, probably neither do we.

And finally, there are the remarks about the food. "These in-flight meals are horrible!"

Whether it is the quality or quantity, I have no say in the matter. The only aspect of the meal I am responsible for is the temperature of the entree. If it's too cold or burnt, then it's my fault. Funny thing is now that many of the flights are non-catered, the same people who complained before, are now complaining of hunger.

Be careful of what you wish for, it might just come true. What's worse than being forced to eat airplane food? Having to pay extra for it.

CHAPTER TWO

10 Unforgettable In-Flight Fights

F or the better part of 18 years, I have witnessed just about every
in-flight fight imaginable. The culprits are many: celebrities, jeal-
ous boyfriends, girlfriends, strangers, friends, inebriates—even
airline employees. However it starts, it never ends in a good way.

You may say it would never happen to you, but consider the following scenario: You are traveling at 35,000 feet, you sit back, relax, and
try to forget the recent hassles with security, weather delays, long lines,
and carry-on mishaps when, all of a sudden, the passenger in front of
you reclines his seat into your lap.

You ask him nicely to raise his seat a couple of inches and he replies
in a "Piss off!" manner. You ask the flight attendant for assistance and
she tells you there is nothing she can do. (Which, unfortunately, is

true: Passengers have the right to recline their seats as far they will go.)

This is the last straw in your long day of unfortunate events, so you decide to make a point of bumping the offending seat as often as possible. Before long, fists are flying.

Unlikely, you think? Think again. Seventy percent of all in-flight fights start with a quarrel over reclining seats. But reclining seats are just one of many excuses for fisticuffs. Here is a list of the top 10 fights I have witnessed in my flying career:

1. A wife caught her husband in the lavatory with another woman. The man had had too much to drink, and there were words. After things calmed down a bit, the wife took all the witnesses' names for future legal proceedings. I guess they settled out of court, as I was never called to testify.

2. A female passenger shoved a wad of chewing gum into the hair of a woman making fun of her hairdo. It was like two cats spinning around in a whirlwind. And these ladies were grown adults, not teenagers.

3. During the meal service, a gentleman asked the reclining passenger in from of him for a few more inches so he could eat. When the recliner rudely said no, the gentleman dumped his entire plate of cheese tortellini directly on top of his head.

4. An Indian man flying from Mumbai became angry when I cut off his alcohol. He took a swing at both me and a pilot, and missed badly. We handcuffed him to the seat. The gentleman was arrested in London and received six months in jail. (That was before 9/11. The charge and penalty would be much stiffer now.)

5. A woman caught her boyfriend flirting with a flight attendant. Later in the flight, the man came to me disheveled and crying, pleading for a different seat. Apparently, every time he fell asleep, the girlfriend punched him in the face.

6. A rude passenger in Business Class, who was yelling at the flight attendant, was the victim of many direct hits with peanuts, which were being fired by an anonymous passenger. Most everyone was

asleep in the cabin, so finding the perpetrator was no easy feat. Eventually, the man caught the culprit in mid-throw: a slovenly young man dressed in shorts and a t-shirt. When he grabbed the young man by the scruff of the neck, he found himself on the floor, brought down by the culprit's bodyguard. The young man turned out to be a famous singer in one of my favorite rock bands. He went on to write a well-known song and music video about commercial air travel.

7. At the gate during a flight delay, a verbally abusive husband took out his frustration on his wife. The crowd and I were forced to listen to this man deliver insult after insult, but after he finally slapped his wife, a nearby female passenger spun him around and delivered a punch that would have made Muhammed Ali proud.

8. A First Class passenger greeted her flight attendant by throwing her fur coat at her and demanding, "Do something with this." The flight attendant replied, "Certainly," then threw the fur coat out the open door and onto the tarmac. The passenger raced up, demanded an explanation and got the reply, "I don't touch fur. Plus, I did something with it as you asked." The passenger slapped the flight attendant, earning herself a night in jail (First Class doesn't give you every privilege), and the flight attendant was eventually fired.

9. Fifteen years ago, a husband-and-wife pilot team had to make an unscheduled landing after a cockpit argument turned physical. I learned this from the husband, now divorced, who is proud to be the man behind the rule that spouses may not fly in the same pilot crew.

10. My most memorable incident was a flight with a fellow flight attendant and friend named Lance. Lance had an effeminate personality and a unique sense of humor. In the boarding area, our muscle-headed first officer ranted on and on about how the flight attendants had better agree to concessions in an ongoing labor negotiation. He was shut down each time by Lance's barbed wit. Not liking being made a fool, he called Lance a "fairy" and gave him a shove. In one swift karate move, Lance spun around and

flipped the first officer on his back. "A fairy who has a black belt," Lance said in his most effeminate voice. "Let's end this now before someone really gets hurt."

The enraged pilot regrouped and charged again. Lance dodged a fist, delivered an elbow to the face and a swift kick to the groin. The pilot fell back again, blood streaming from his nose. The passengers and I watched in disbelief.

Security arrived moments later and the two were escorted away. At Lance's request, I took names and addresses of eyewitnesses. I was interviewed, wrote many reports and was called to testify at a disciplinary hearing. I did all that I could, but Lance was fired. The kicker: Even though the pilot started it, he was only suspended.

Remarkably, Lance took it all in stride. He filed a lawsuit against the airline for false dismissal and after two years settled out of court for job reinstatement, back pay, and an undisclosed amount of money.

After his first month back to work, Lance called to tell me he had quit. He had planned to go back to school at the time of the incident anyway, and the pilot had unwittingly provided him with the opportunity and, eventually, the tuition money. Lance had once taken some pre-law courses; during his lawsuit he passed the bar exam and became a full-fledged lawyer.

"Lance, I don't know what to say. You're like..., like...," I said.

"I know, I know, kind of like Super Fairy, right?" Lance interjected.

"Yeah!"

Lance was the winner of that fight, hands down.

CHAPTER THREE

10 Costumes That Won't Fly

O n Halloween, most airline crew members are allowed to wear a costume to work. Some costumes are elaborate and well thought out, while others look like a last-minute throw-together. Sometimes passengers get into the spirit and dress up as well. Every year there is someone—a passenger or a crew member—who takes dress-up a little too far.

The following are costumes that I have actually seen at the airport, along with the consequences that followed.

1. **Osama bin Laden.** Maybe funny at a college frat party, but a little too close to the bone at the airport. The person who did this was— believe it or not—a pilot, and let's just say it went over like a lead

balloon. I laughed, not at his costume but at his surprise when he discovered the authorities didn't think it was funny.

2. **Drunken pilot.** A passenger thought it would be clever to come to the airport dressed up as a pilot and hit the bars a good three hours before his flight. He met up with several passengers who were horrified when he claimed to be their pilot. He wasn't breaking any rules, and nobody had the right to tell him to quit, although security was alerted and made sure he wasn't really working the flight.

3. **Police officer.** Impersonating a law enforcement officer is illegal no matter what day it is, and with cameras and real cops all over the terminal, if you turn up in this costume, you are just a chicken waiting to be plucked.

4. **Airline CEO.** I wish I had thought of this one. A flight attendant dressed up as the tycoon from the Monopoly game and added a badge identifying himself as an airline CEO. He bragged about his pension during the whole flight, threw fake money around, and laughed continuously at the other airline employees. Simple, yet brilliant.

5. **Flasher.** It may sound like a good idea, but keep in mind that indecency laws are strictly enforced. When a man from Florida wearing nothing but a trench coat flashed the women as he passed through the terminal, he was arrested. Apparently, he had been arrested before on the same charge, so maybe it wasn't a Halloween costume after all.

6. **Mass murderer.** Dressing up as an infamous murderer in a public place, especially in an airport, is also a bad idea. On my flights I have seen Lizzie Borden, Son of Sam, and Jack the Ripper. The best one was a flight attendant dressed up as a box of Cheerios carrying a fake sword. I am embarrassed to say it but, yes, he was a Cereal Killer.

7. **Suicide bomber.** Not funny, period! Two flight attendants dressed up as "Spy vs. Spy" characters but ended up looking like terrorists with bombs. They were suspended when a couple of passengers raised a ruckus.

8. **Anything explosive.** Two gate agents actually dressed as bombs with a lit fuse. They worked the customer service desk and anytime anyone got angry, they would reply, "Be careful, I am operating with a short fuse today." Surprisingly enough, the costume went over well, or I guess you could say that it didn't bomb. Still, I wouldn't recommend this stunt at the airport, especially these days.

9. **Priest.** A colleague of mine offended an actual priest with his "Father Ted" outfit. It wasn't the costume that was the problem; it was the Catholic jokes that came with it.

10. **The opposite sex.** You may wear a dress as a gag on Halloween, which might make some people chuckle, but before you know it, you are sneaking out to catch the cosmetic sales at the duty-free shop.

11. **Any character of ethnic origin.** Don Juan, a matador, sumo wrestler, geisha girl, Rastafarian (especially if you're white), etc. You have to realize that Halloween is an American tradition, but when you are in an airport, you may come into contact with international passengers who could take great offense.

12. **Feminine hygiene product.** A man showed up at a New York airport dressed as a tampon. In fact, he made most people, including me, laugh out loud. However, small children kept asking their parents what he was, and I doubt the flustered parents were inclined to begin sex education at such a young age, much less at an airport. The costume also had drawbacks for the wearer; for example, sitting on the airplane was difficult, and he had to take his cotton top off because he was blocking the video screen.

Next time you're flying on Halloween, wear a costume that will put a little smile on a crew member's face. As long as it isn't one of the previously mentioned get-ups, it might get you a free drink on the airplane. I have known many gate agents who have upgraded as many costumed passengers as would fit in First Class. It's in the spirit of *"Trick or treat!"* and all those grinning jack o'-lanterns.

CHAPTER FOUR

High Expectations

D oes the happy glow of pregnancy still glow when you fly on an airplane? Or does it fade at the first sight of cramped seats and crying children? My wife has some opinions on this subject. She's an airplane pilot, and she continued flying during the first part of her pregnancy.

But, first, she wants to set something straight.

"Happy glow?" she asks. "If you want to call hemorrhoids, low bladder capacity, frequent indigestion, and a constant backache a condition of 'happy glowing,' then you are definitely—a man."

She was feeling somewhat more chipper when we flew off for one last romantic holiday before the baby was due. We knew what was in store the following February—a Diaper Genie and 2 a.m. feedings—so we ventured off to the Big Island of Hawaii for some sun and relaxation.

I brought pen and paper along, thinking this would be the perfect opportunity to write about the future of our lives and the shape of things to come.

Trying very hard to ignore the crying baby behind us, we settled into our flight—me with my wine and my wife with her milk—and we wrote out these 10 tips together:

1. **Ask your doctor.** First and foremost, get your physician's OK to fly. Our doctor gave us the green light to travel between the second and eighth months, provided there were no complications. Your doctor may have a different opinion.

2. **Stop at the drug store.** Bring along some antacids, extra-strength Tylenol and Preparation H. You may be feeling fine on the way to the airport, but once you take your cramped seat in the stuffy cabin, your body may decide to rebel.

3. **Get up and dance.** Force yourself to get up every couple of hours to stretch, walk, or waddle around. Do whatever it takes to keep the blood flowing.

4. **Pack snacks.** The airlines aren't serving much in the way of food these days, and it could be several hours before you eat anything substantial, so bring a back-up food supply. Luckily, we brought quite a bit of food with us, as there was no meal service for the entire eight-hour flight. (I am a flight attendant, and that appalled even me.) My wife highly recommends Fig Newtons.

5. **Drink fluids.** Drink lots of water but dilute it with 10 percent fruit juice. This way, rather than visiting the lavatory every 15 minutes, you'll be going every 30 minutes instead. Believe me, that's a big difference.

6. **Take a seat.** Speaking of going, you will want an aisle seat as close to the lavatory as possible. If you don't get the aisle seat, tell the passengers seated in your row that you will need to move around a lot during the flight; maybe someone will switch seats with you. If not, feel no guilt about getting up as often as you need to. After all, they were warned.

7. **Ask for help.** If you need help with your bags, or you need any special assistance at all, don't be afraid to ask. And, please, if you feel anything is wrong or out of the ordinary, ask the flight attendant to call for a doctor. I once had an expectant mother on a flight who went into early labor; a doctor on-board was able to stop the labor, thus avoiding a premature delivery.

8. **Check your bags.** Stowing your luggage in the overhead compartment is a tricky business in the best of circumstances, so skip the hassles and check it in. You're in no hurry, so let someone else lug your baggage. Twenty pounds is about all you should lift when you're pregnant, and we both know your bags weigh more than that.

9. **Build in some wait time.** No amount of encouragement can get a pregnant woman to move faster, not even a final boarding call, so allow more time than usual between connecting flights. Tip for husbands: Don't tell your wife she reminds you of *The March of the Penguins* as she makes her way through the terminal. I learned this the hard way when I got a hard elbow to the gut.

10. **Establish some boundaries.** For some reason, people on airplanes are just dying to tell pregnant women the gruesome details of their own birthing experiences. When someone starts off with a story, just say, "No gory stories, please!" Similarly, if you don't want strangers patting your belly, just say so. People mean well but, really, you're not public property.

When we got to Hawaii, my wife and I slept for a day and a half, but eventually we enjoyed our romantic getaway. One curious note is that when we were snorkeling, turtles swam up and surrounded my wife; they seemed fascinated and protective at the same time.

Love takes on a special meaning when you see your wife, seven months pregnant, waddling down a beach in search of a snorkeling adventure. Seeing her heading out to sea in her black-and-white swimsuit reminded me of the penguin movie again, but this time I kept it to myself.

CHAPTER FIVE

Strangers in the Flight

I f you fly often enough, sooner or later you will sit next to a passenger you can't stand. There are the complainers, the opinionated, the loud and obnoxious, those with unusual quirks or phobias, people with screaming babies, and others with gas. You name it, and I have probably sat next to it at one time or another.

I wrote this while sitting next to the classic nightmare seatmate. After announcing his importance to the world by constantly using his cell phone, he managed to annoy everyone around him with his loud and incredibly embarrassing points of view. He drank too much, spoke too often and pretty much complained his way across the Atlantic. I hoped that he would eventually glance over my shoulder and see himself in the column I was writing, but unfortunately he never did.

I usually consider a flight next to a stranger a chance to delve into another person's outlook. The inspiration for most of my writing comes from such opportunities, but, to be honest, there are times when I just want to be left alone and relax in my own private world. Those are the times that my neighbors get on my nerves. Take these people, for instance. Do you recognize any of them?

- **Mr. High Flyer.** This gentleman complained about everything during the first half of the flight. When he discovered that I am a flight attendant, he decided to complain to me the rest of the way.

- **Miss Fear Of Flying.** This poor soul burst into floods of tears during the taxi out, and it only got worse after that. It was a nine-hour flight.

- **Mr. Freaky.** This middle-aged man stared at a picture of a boy, chanted, and swatted at imaginary flies the entire flight.

- **Mr. Itchy.** This fellow either had a bad case of jock itch or was—well, let's just say he was feeling a bit crabby. By the end of the flight I was feeling itchy myself, but maybe that was just my imagination.

- **Ms. Drinks Too Much.** First she tried to get me to join the Mile High Club with her, then she started talking to herself. Eventually she needed to use both our sick bags.

- **Mr. Politically Incorrect.** This United States senator let me know he had no respect for stewardesses or female pilots. I waited until our second drink to tell him that I am a flight attendant and my wife is a pilot.

- **Mr. Gassy.** This gentleman made no attempt to disguise the matter that was rotting inside his intestines, even though the restroom was vacant the entire time. Talk about airing your problems! Another gentleman, Mr. Smelly Feet, comes in a distant second, though I must say his were the worst feet my olfactory passages have ever encountered.

- **Ms. Not-Contagious.** Now, how does anyone ever know that they are not contagious? This was her claim, but she sneezed, coughed, and wiped her nose throughout the flight. Needless to say, I came down with her cold two days later.

- **Mr. Nose-Picker.** If this man were to embark on a career of nostril mining, he would be a huge success. Unfortunately, I have peripheral vision and I couldn't help witnessing the whole booger-extraction expedition.

- **Mr. Multi-Tasker.** This fellow was a claustrophobe who also had Parkinson's disease *and* Tourette's syndrome. No joke. We actually became quite good friends, which just goes to show that you should give your seat neighbor a chance. I'm sure you're not always a joy to sit next to, either.

So what is the decent, well-mannered traveler to do when stuck with a difficult seatmate? Here are 10 tips:

1. **Move it.** If the flight is not full, you don't have to suffer through the entire journey in your assigned seat. Get up and move to another seat; either ask a flight attendant to find you a different seat or locate one yourself. The person who was enjoying two seats may roll their eyes a bit, but he'll get over it.

2. **Bring earplugs.** My favorite standard amenity comes up aces again. Just make sure your seatmate sees you plug in, or he'll be talking at you the whole flight anyway. Are there such things as nose plugs? If it is a smelly situation, put some mild, fragrant lotion under your nostrils and point your air vent toward the source of the problem.

3. **Lie if you have to.** Don't let your seatmate know what you do for a living, especially if you work for an airline. I know it sounds dishonest, but how many questions about your field of expertise do you really want to answer in your time off? Instead, make up a conversation-stopping occupation. Insurance salesman or data processor usually does the trick.

4. **Talk it out.** Try to converse with the person. Annoying people can be interesting, too (my friend with Tourette's certainly was).

5. **Find a way out of the conversation.** If your seatmate turns out not to be interesting, or if she's just an overly chatty person, fake a yawn and then pretend to sleep. Alternatively, you could just tell her that you aren't in the mood for conversation, but this direct approach may be taken for rudeness, and then you're stuck with an icy relationship for the entire flight.

6. **Phone it in.** If you have an in-flight phone at your seat, take it out of the cradle and pretend to make a phone call. In a loud conversational voice explain to your imaginary friend on the other end that you are sitting near a complete moron. He usually gets the message, and the announcement gives the others around you a good chuckle.

7. **Look on the bright side.** Don't like your seatmate? Take heart. Odds are, you'll never see him again.

8. **Go a little crazy.** You could pretend you are mentally deranged and try to scare off the offending neighbor with a bit of bizarre behavior, but be careful not to overdo it, as you might get taken off the flight.

9. **Fight another day.** If you find the atmosphere getting hostile, avoid any direct confrontation. Instead, notify a flight attendant. I was once pretty close to telling the guy next to me where he could stick his cell phone, but my rational side prevailed.

10. **Sympathize with your fellow man.** Realize that some people are not at their best while flying: mothers with infants, fearful flyers, folks who have just been laid off—you name it. Chances are you've been a less-than-perfect seatmate once or twice yourself, so cut your neighbor some slack.

Some of the most interesting people I have ever met are passengers that I had dreaded sitting next to. But then again, some made my Worst Nightmare list. Each flight is a crapshoot. You just never know who will turn up.

CHAPTER SIX

Plane Spooky

With the celebration of Halloween comes the telling of ghost stories. They usually contain bizarre, unexplained, and the of-tentimes unbelievable coincidences that send shivers up one's spine. Mine concern the spooky happenings in the realm of air travel, and while I can't confirm every one of the stories, all are very much alive in the world of flight crews.

I got the idea for this chapter while I was working an all-nighter last Halloween. The crew gathered in the back galley and told air travel ghost stories. We dimmed the lights and kept our voices low so the sleeping passengers wouldn't hear us. The following are the top 13 spooky stories. Trick or treat!

1. A 72-year-old flight attendant (yes, she really was 72) always insisted that someday she would die on a layover in Italy. One day she arrived at the terminal to work her usual flight to Rome, but she was sent home because the flight had been canceled. She passed away the very next day. You see, canceled flights can ruin a flight attendant's plans, too.

2. An especially bizarre story involves a young flight attendant whose family persuaded her to retire after the Lockerbie tragedy. It seems her mother had dreamed her daughter would die in an airplane disaster. The young woman became an accountant, and after years of promotions went to work for a firm in New York. Her office was in the World Trade Center, and she perished on 9/11.

3. When a pair of elderly newlyweds went to Europe for their honeymoon, the husband had a heart attack and died. The wife arranged to have his body brought back in a casket to their new home in Florida. She made the connecting flight but the casket did not; in fact, the airline could not locate it for five days. When the casket was finally found, at the deceased's hometown airport, it was . . . empty! One way or another, that man got cold feet.

4. A flight to Europe took off with a crew of four pilots and landed with only three. During a break, one of the pilots wandered off and was never heard from again. The authorities took apart the plane but have yet to solve the case. Authorities determined that the pilot had been suffering from depression and was behind on his alimony payments; they surmised he had slipped off the airplane disguised as a passenger in hopes of starting a new life. But there is no record of him going through customs or immigration, and his bags were all still on-board.

5. Many tales of 9/11 coincidences seem to be in circulation these days. The one I find a bit uncanny tells of a father who discussed fears of dying with his son the day before his son was scheduled to fly. His son died on American Airlines Flight 77, which crashed into the western side of the Pentagon, where, incredibly enough, the father worked (that very side). The father survived. He had taken a rare day off to play a game of golf.

6. Several years ago, a flight crashed shortly after take-off. When authorities recovered the black box, they found that the pilots' last conversation was about the dating habits of the flight attendants working that day. A few years later, two pilots and an off-duty crew member were talking about the details of that tragedy in the cockpit of their own flight just before take-off. They remarked on how hard it must be for families to hear those final words. Shortly after take-off, their own flight crashed, leaving no survivors. The last sentence was, "So we had better make our conversations good for our families." I listened to the black box audio of that flight on the Internet, and am sorry now that I did, as it has haunted me ever since.

7. What about the flight attendant who discovered that her husband, a pilot, was cheating with countless co-workers? The husband mysteriously disappeared, but the investigation was not highly publicized, perhaps because of this unsavory coincidence: The pilot's body was never found, but the flight attendant was famous for bringing homemade sandwiches to work, then generously handing them out to passengers and crew when there was no scheduled meal service. Talk about getting rid of the evidence!

8. I once flew a 767 with an all-male crew of nine flight attendants. Remarkably, all the flight attendants were heterosexual and married. What made this so weird was that both of the male pilots were gay. If you know the airline business, you know that this is truly a one in a million chance.

9. Quite a few years back, before my time, a man shot his gun into the air signaling the end of duck season. The shot pierced a commercial airplane flying overhead, and some pellets hit a passenger in the bottom. The investigation revealed that the victim was, unbelievably, the brother of the man who fired the gun. This story is hard to believe, I grant you.

10. I also remember the story about a superstitious flight attendant who followed strict rules of numerology. She would seldom trade her trips, not wanting to alter fate, and she never went against her readings. So, when offered a trade for one December flight, she

declined, even though it would suit her Christmas schedule better. Sadly, that was her last flight: Pan Am Flight 103, which crashed over Lockerbie, Scotland.

11. Two male pilots lost their jobs for flying naked. Apparently, they were playing a joke on one of the flight attendants and it backfired when the wrong crew member entered the cockpit. This may not qualify as the spookiest story, but the mental image is haunting enough.

12. Not telling her husband that she was joining him on his European layover, this pilot's wife took Seat 1A in First Class as a romantic surprise. What she didn't know was that sitting next to her in 1B was her husband's mistress. After take-off, he saw them both, and you should have seen his expression. I hear that the wife and the mistress became good friends. I also hear the pilot is paying a lot in alimony.

13. Stopped by the police for speeding on the way to the airport, a woman missed her flight. The airplane crashed and there were no survivors. What makes this story really strange is that the standby passenger who took her place was related to the police officer who gave the woman the ticket. It does have a romantic ending, however, as the police officer and the lucky lady were married two years later. That is one relationship that fate definitely had a hand in. Some luck is just plane spooky.

CHAPTER SEVEN

Love is in the Air

I recently flew with a senior flight attendant who told me that she joined the Mile High Club 35 years ago with a total stranger on Valentine's Day, and has been married to him ever since. She says it's not a total coincidence that her son is also 35 and named John.

The Mile High Club, for those of you who aren't frequent fliers, is an exclusive society for those who have consummated their relationship at cruising altitude.

I remember back to the first time I witnessed it while working a flight. I was in my second year and had a bit more confidence in playing the good sport with the passengers.

I caught a passenger slyly sneaking into an already-occupied lavatory. I rushed up to First Class, popped open a bottle of champagne, grabbed some flowers, made a make-shift membership card, and rushed back to the scene. There I stood, with a goofy wide smile, ready to embarrass the new inductees.

A few minutes passed and out came two male passengers. I froze, and in shock I dropped the bottle and caught a champagne shower. I was young, naive and truly not expecting that to happen.

An attractive lady approached me once and informed me if I upgraded her to First Class, she would guarantee my membership in the club immediately. Luckily, First Class was full, so I had a valid excuse. Is First Class really worth it? In her case, I guess it was.

Once there was a young woman afraid of flying, who decided to relieve her fear by drinking. Not accustomed to alcohol, her inhibitions vanished, and she was caught in the lavatory twice with two different men. I'm sure a sleeping pill would have been more effective—and less embarrassing.

One Valentine's Day flight the lavatory call light was blinking and sounding off rhythmically. The crew all looked at each other and wondered if it could be . . . *naah*. We investigated anyway. Moans were coming from the toilet on the left side.

"Are you OK?" we asked in a low voice, but no response came from the lavatory. The bell kept on ringing, but at a faster pace. We opened the door, as we are required to do, and found two new members of the Mile High Club, stark naked, not realizing that they were bumping against the call button.

The lady spotted us first and began to scream. The man whispered, "Shh, somebody will hear us!"

The sensation is supposedly 10 times more intense due to the cabin pressure and the altitude of the airplane. More likely it is because of the excitement of possibly getting caught or doing it in a public place—or so I'm told.

And no, the restroom isn't the only place it's done. The action can take place under a blanket on a night flight, heads bobbing, hands not in sight. Or the lower kitchen galley, the bunkroom, and now I hear Virgin Airways is coming out with double beds in Upper Class. It makes me wonder how they will promote *that* product!

I've even heard of it happening in the cockpit. There was a recent incident where two male pilots and a flight attendant were suspended for a supposed threesome up-front in-flight. Now the logistics of that are puzzling especially since it was on a smaller regional aircraft. They got caught when a pass-riding flight attendant, who happened to be best friends with the wife of one of the pilots, listened in and reported them. Takes the term auto-pilot to a whole new level, doesn't it?

I always get asked if I am a member. Well, there was this one time... Then again, some things should stay between a husband and wife.

My 90-year-old grandmother once asked me about the Mile High Club. She had heard the term, and thought it was some sort of frequent flier club, good towards mileage points. I explained as delicately as possible.

"Sex in an airplane bathroom!" she exclaimed. "Why that's impossible, I've been in one, and there isn't enough room to brush your hair, much less lie down."

CHAPTER EIGHT

Prejudice in the Air

The captain had advised us that our landing at LAX might be a difficult one. We were offered an alternate airport because of the fires and rioting taking place downtown. I couldn't bring myself to believe it was actually happening. It had to be mostly news hype, I thought, an attempt to make the Rodney King verdict appear more sensational.

But just before landing I was called into the cockpit, where I stared in disbelief at the smoke billowing from the ground. Against the setting sun, the smoke cast a grim glow around the so-called "City of Angels."

After we landed, the crew was taken to an airport hotel instead of the usual one downtown. Nobody on the hotel bus said a word, as shock dominated our thoughts. The streets were empty and the area around the airport looked like a ghost town. We got our keys and disappeared to our rooms, hoping CNN would shine a better light on the scene. No one made layover plans, as very few felt like leaving their rooms, much less the hotel. Before that moment, I had never looked upon a person's skin color as a mark of difference. It was a shameful time for all of us.

Fortunately—and unfortunately—the average airline employee is just a number. No classification by color, religion, gender or sexual preference—just a file number with a security clearance. This is not to say that prejudice does not exist in the airline industry. Whenever you put a variety of cultures together in one workplace, biases are bound to surface.

Here are some of the more prevalent forms of prejudice you find in air travel, along with some tips for staying open-minded and courteous when you travel.

1. **Sexism.** My wife, who is a pilot, tells me of passengers boarding the airplane and asking her for a drink; they see the gender, not the uniform. When one man discovered that she was not only a pilot but also the captain, he retrieved his bags and took another flight. Come on, hasn't he ever heard of brains *and* beauty?

2. **Assumptions.** Not only do most people assume that I am a pilot, but when I tell them I am a flight attendant, they assume I am gay—which I'm not, either (not that there is anything wrong with being gay). Assumptions are inevitable, but try to keep an open mind. You might be surprised by what sneaks in.

3. **Religion.** If someone is dressed according to their religious custom—or if they're kneeling and praying in the back of the airplane—mind your business and allow that person some privacy. A female passenger once approached me during boarding to report that the man next to her was chanting terrorist phrases from a book. It turns out he was reading the Quran. Not all Muslims are terrorists, just as not every Catholic priest is a pedophile.

4. **Rich and famous.** If you see somebody famous at the airport or on the airplane and they are being reclusive or seem rude, realize that they have probably encountered many gawkers and fans in

the course of the day and have grown weary of them. The shyest celebrity I ever served onboard was David Letterman. Of course, I greeted him like a long lost buddy. He didn't appreciate the attention and seemed ill at ease the entire flight, which was undoubtedly my fault.

5. **Skin color.** Occasionally, you get a crew member telling an off-color racist joke. It's one of those jokes they tell right after looking around to see if the coast is clear. There is no room in the cabin for racist views, and the people who openly express them don't last very long. Of course, racism isn't limited to crew members. I was on a flight one time when a passenger whispered in my ear, "Do you realize that you are the only white member of the crew?" I stopped, looked up and down the aisle, smiled and took pride in the fact that I really hadn't noticed.

6. **Watch what you say.** A black female flight attendant was working hard in the back galley when a passenger waiting for the bathroom teasingly asked her, "Are you the galley slave?" Realizing that his idle comment could be misconstrued as a racist remark, the passenger instantly apologized. No offense intended—and none taken—but why take a chance? Think before you speak. That episode reminds me of a time many years ago, when I was in the Army. I went to see a movie on the base. There were two fairly long lines for two different shows: *The Color Purple*, and *Indiana Jones*. At the back of the line I innocently asked, "Is this the line for *The Color People*?" Everyone in line turned around in disbelief. "Purple!" I cried. "I meant purple!" It was just a slip of the tongue, but I certainly deserved a crack on the head, and I went to see *Indiana Jones* just to be safe.

7. **Sensitivity training.** I believe in educating the public about the realities of modern-day prejudices, but I also believe there should be limits on the content. Should I really say, "Coffee plain" instead of "Black" and "Coffee regular" instead of "White"? Do the people who design these courses ever confer with the groups whom they feel we might be offending?

8. **Security profiling.** Airline management tells us to look out for anyone suspicious. Now this doesn't mean everyone of Middle Eastern descent or anyone wearing a turban, but not surprisingly these are the people who are most often pointed out for secondary screening. It's not called ethnic profiling, but what is the reality? Let's face it: Ever since the 9/11 attacks and the ongoing conflict in Iraq, there has been a dramatic rise in fear and hostility directed against those of Arab descent. When these people are singled out for special scrutiny, is it caution or is it prejudice?

I hope we Americans take a hard look at lingering prejudices of all kinds. We are a wonderful nation of differences, a meeting ground for hundreds of great cultures, heritages, and ways of life. We need to celebrate those differences, and a good way to begin is to remember that we all came from somewhere else. Every race is a guest here, and each should be made to feel welcome.

As Rodney King himself asked, "Can't we all just get along?"

I say: Let's try a little harder to do just that.

CHAPTER NINE

The Flying Hypochondriac

I guess you could say I'm a hypochondriac. As a kid, I was always looking up new ailments in the library after school. Over the years, I imagined I'd contracted everything from cancer to meningitis. As I got older, I learned to laugh at this obsession. I imagined joining a 12-step program—call it Hypochondriacs Anonymous—where I would stand up and say, "Hello, my name is James and I am a hypochondriac. It has been two months since my last fatal illness, and I have not been to see a doctor in at least three days, even though I'm pretty sure I'm dying of something again."

Even perfectly reasonable people can be squeamish about air travel, what with SARS, bird flu, tuberculosis, and smallpox all making recent airline news. I remember flying into Asia during the SARS epidemic. The flight attendants were handing out face masks—and wearing them, too—so pretty soon the 747 looked like some epidemic movie gone bad. I got to my layover hotel and actually started feeling and seeing some symptoms of the illness. Your mind has a vivid imagination; given free rein, it will see what it wants to see.

My minor case of hypochondria never really interfered with my life until the day I diagnosed myself—correctly—with food-borne Hepatitis A. (There is nothing worse for a hypochondriac than a self-diagnosis that turns out to be correct.) I recovered, but I started taking many more health precautions and became more aware of my surroundings. As the old saying goes, "Once bitten, twice shy."

I know, you're probably thinking that my career is a poor choice for a hypochondriac. As a flight attendant, I am constantly around large groups of people, some of whom are sick, and I'm usually stuck inside a metal tube with a filtration system that basically mixes body fluids with cabin moisture. Maybe you're right. Maybe this is the wrong job. But maybe my experiences can help you become more aware of your health when you're flying. That would be a good thing. So here are some tips to keep in mind when flying, whether you're a hypochondriac or not:

1. **Paper towels.** When you go to the restroom, grab a paper towel and use that as a glove for the duration of your stay, never directly touching anything. It's quick, easy, and hygienic.

2. **Vaccines.** The best way to protect against the more dreadful diseases associated with international travel is to be properly immunized. Do your research and get the shot. I wish I had.

3. **Clean hands.** You don't need to shake everyone's hand, especially during cold and flu season. But if you do, wash your hands before touching your face.

4. **Antibacterial gels.** You can't always wash your hands, but antibacterial gels now come in handy travel-sized bottles.

5. **Listen to your body.** If you pay close enough attention, you can tell when you are starting to get sick. Don't ignore the whispered warnings. There are many products out there containing zinc that are said to prevent colds and speed along recovery—provided

they are taken at the earliest sign of illness. Personally, I swear by Zicam.

6. **Mind your feet.** Never, never—I repeat, never!—walk around an airplane with bare feet, and don't let your children do it either. I can't tell you how many people I see going to the restroom with no shoes on, and God only knows what's on that floor.

7. **Watch out for water.** Tap water, ice, and even raw vegetables are risky when you travel abroad. Stick to bottled water and refrain from any uncooked food that comes into direct contact with water. Sorry, but this does include salads.

8. **Don't chance the cheap.** If it doesn't look like a hygienic place to eat from the front room, you can bet the kitchen situation is worse. Pay a little extra for the peace of mind. And trust me when I say: Stay away from foreign food stands.

9. **Love thy neighbor.** But if he looks sick and is sitting right next to you on the airplane, politely move to another seat. That move could save your vacation.

10. **Don't obsess.** You don't need gloves and a mask when you're traveling—much less a hat to ward off solar radiation. You just need a little common sense.

No longer am I embarrassed by my health precautions. In fact, they are second nature to me now, because I never again want to go through two long months of night sweats and exhaustion as I did with Hepatitis A. I don't consider myself a full-blown hypochondriac, but if I do die of some strange malady, I want my tombstone to read: "Ha! I told you there was something wrong with me!"

CHAPTER TEN

You Make the Call

E very day, flight attendants face difficult decisions that have no
real precedent. Just look at the recent incident in which a United
Airlines passenger went to the lavatory and hanged himself. The
logistics of how he accomplished this—not to mention why—are a bit
puzzling (though I have been in a few airplane toilets that made me
want to cry). What would you have done had you been the flight attendant who discovered the body?

In the 18 years that I have been flying, I have faced many tough
decisions. Some I handled well, some not so well. After a difficult incident, people are happy to tell you how they think it should have been
resolved. I am going to present you with 10 situations and ask you, the
passenger, to make the call. The way each was actually handled—correctly or incorrectly—is given at the end of the list.

1. A male passenger plays a pornographic DVD on a portable player. I notice there are children within sight and that other passengers are becoming annoyed. When I ask the gentleman to put the DVD away, he refuses, citing his personal rights. What do I do?

2. A female passenger, acting strangely and smelling of alcohol, asks for another drink. I decide she's had too much already and cut her off. She informs me that she is not drunk but has multiple sclerosis and would still like that drink. Do I serve her?

3. On a long international flight, a First Class passenger airs his intestines continuously. I mean, he passes gas big time. It gets so bad that most everyone has a tissue stuffed up his nose, and a couple of passengers are getting sick. One flight attendant decides to go on a smell hunt and tracks down the culprit. Should she say something?

4. A male passenger is reading a book on how to build bombs. The title is in large print, and surrounding passengers become alarmed. Should a flight attendant do something?

5. A couple joining the Mile High Club in one of the lavatories makes their intentions clear by vocalizing loudly. You knock on the door, hoping they will either stop or become more discreet. When they don't stop and passengers start to complain, what do you do?

6. You find a roll of money on the floor of the lavatory. It carries no identification. You count it and find it totals well over $500. Your paycheck has recently been cut and you could really use that windfall. What do you do?

7. A female passenger comes to the galley and tells you that her husband has just passed away. The couple knew this might happen, as the man had a serious heart condition. There are no empty seats to which he can be moved, and you know that if you report the death before landing, all the passengers will be quarantined for several hours. What do you do?

8. You are on an eight-hour flight that has been delayed for two hours due to mechanical trouble. When it finally takes off, you get a note from Operations saying that everyone on-board will miss their

connecting flights. Do you tell the passengers right away, knowing that everyone will be put in a foul mood, or do you wait until
nearer the end of the flight? Or do you not tell them at all?

9. A passenger boards wearing an extremely racist T-shirt. Having
    had several complaints from passengers during boarding, and
    fearing World War III could break out in-flight, what do you do—
    if anything?

10. One of your pilots is late and boards in a hurry, smelling of alco-
    hol. He is not acting peculiarly, but the smell is obvious. How do
    you handle the situation?

The solution to these dilemmas is not always straightforward, and
different people may handle them differently. The following, right or
wrong, is how each was in fact resolved.

1. I confiscated the DVD player and returned it after the flight. The
    passenger took my name and employee number and promised a
    lawsuit. Yes, I do believe in rights—everybody's rights. Two years
    later, I have yet to hear of a lawsuit.

2. There was no way I could determine if this lady did indeed have
    MS. I kindly refused the drink, citing my responsibility to moni-
    tor onboard alcohol consumption.

3. I believe the brave flight attendant who did the investigating went
    beyond the call of duty. In the end, she did say something, as it
    had gotten to the point of making people ill. The passenger con-
    fessed but said there was nothing he could do. The flight attendant
    directed him to a restroom that had not been utilized, where he
    was able to air out his laundry more appropriately.

4. I had no problem telling the man to either put the book away or
    hold it more discreetly. It was a no-brainer after 9/11.

5. The knocking did not help so I unlocked the door. Conveniently,
    this action automatically turns off the light. The couple got the
    hint and curtailed their activities. My next step would have been
    to open the door. No, not because I am a voyeur, but because she

was a screamer and the other passengers were getting annoyed.

6. I made an announcement that something valuable had been found in the forward lavatory but I omitted any description. An elderly lady came up to me almost in tears saying she had lost her money. I happily returned it, feeling guilty that I had entertained other plans for it. When she gave me a $2 reward, the guilt quickly disappeared.

7. Nothing was done until after landing, when we officially "discovered" the death. The wife, who had pretended her husband was asleep, was grateful that no spectacle had been made.

8. The purser decided to delay the bad news, which ended up being the right move. The pilots had made up much of the time in-flight, and half the passengers were able to make their connections after all.

9. I greeted the passenger in a kind but firm tone, saying, "You can wear something over your shirt, turn it inside out, or get off." He quickly reversed it and said nothing the remainder of the flight.

10. I spoke to the other pilot and told him of my concern. It turned out that someone had spilled a drink on the pilot, who was willing to take an alcohol test if I so wished. There were no hard feelings, and he changed his shirt. I think both sides handled that one well.

How did you do? Did you make the same calls? What would you have done differently?

CHAPTER ELEVEN

The Flag of Our Youth

I have been working military charters for most of my career as a flight attendant. My first military charter was in the early 1990s, when such flights usually supported some lightning-strike mission to get some evil dictator out of some unheard-of country. On that first occasion, I went to Rome for three weeks and worked a shuttle delivering soldiers to Saudi Arabia. I was young and single, eager to see the world and happy for another excuse to party in Italy.

Fifteen years later, the military charters continue to fly and, remarkably enough, often to the same area of the world. But it's not as easy for me to work the military flights these days. The troops seem to be getting younger and fear is rife on every flight. The soldiers have spent months preparing to go to Iraq or Afghanistan, and they've spent the last week saying goodbye to their families, but it isn't until they get on the airplane and take off that the reality really sinks in.

Their expressions tell it all: *"How did I get here?"* they seem to say. And, *"Oh my God, am I really going off to war?"*

True, these soldiers have all volunteered for their service, but I'm sure most of them never believed it would actually come to this. I certainly never did. When I was in the military, back in the 1980s, my job was to play the trumpet in Germany. I couldn't afford college, and the Army was the only way I could get a degree. But I never feared for my life. After all, nobody was going to mess with the United States of America. War? I never gave it a second thought.

Times change, and now I find working these charters get tougher with every journey. Not physically, for the flights are in fact very easy. No alcohol is served, the soldiers are very polite, and most of them just want to sleep. It's the mental and emotional strain that weigh me down. I recently completed another military charter, and I returned to the States with a heavy heart. The young men and women had filed onto the airplane wearing their fresh, new uniforms and brave faces. But underneath they harbored those looks of disbelief.

A 19-year-old boy pulled me aside.

"Is this like another Vietnam conflict?" he asked me. "What do I do if I am not up to this?"

I tried to reassure him, but I had no clear-cut answers.

Remarkably, I also ran into a friend and fellow Army bandsman on that flight. I did a double take.

"Freddy, is that you?" I exclaimed.

"Wysong? What are you doing on this plane?"

We talked over old times, about how his trombone got traded in for an M-16 during the first Gulf War. He said the band had changed. It wasn't like the old days, when we performed at German beer festivals. This was his third and final tour of duty in Iraq; when he was done, he would retire. He mused that I had made the right choice in getting out, but I joked with him not to be so sure, as he was still young and about to retire with a nice monthly check from the Army. At least his CEO couldn't rob him of his pension like mine did.

It was the only bright spot in an otherwise dreary mission. As we touched down at our destination, the young soldier across from me vainly fought off tears. Soon they were streaming down his face.

I usually look forward to bringing the soldiers home—so much more gratifying—than taking them off to war. But this time there were no troops aboard the return flight—a clear indication that there would be no early end to the conflict.

Not long after I got back, I worked a civilian flight from Germany. Upon boarding, a grumpy-looking First Class passenger insisted on speaking to the purser, who unfortunately was yours truly. From the look on his face, I figured the gentleman was getting ready to complain about something.

"What can I do for you, sir?" I asked, putting on my defensive shield.

"I'd like you to go back to Economy and pick a service member coming back from Iraq and give him my seat," he said.

For the first time in a long time I was speechless. I actually felt on the verge of tears. Not only was I wrong about this man, but I suddenly felt the greatest admiration for him. I did as he requested, but made sure I kept him amply supplied with First Class wine the entire flight. The soldier who got his seat had a kid-in-a-candy-store smile on his face the whole flight. My heart and my faith were renewed.

No matter what our political views are, the troops need and deserve our support. Next Thanksgiving, give thanks to our boys, girls, fathers, and mothers who are away in some foreign place so we can be safe in our holiday homes. If you see some soldiers at the airport, shake their hands, pat them on the back, buy them a coffee, and, whatever you do, don't forget to thank them for their service.

PART FOUR

Fellow Passengers

CHAPTER ONE

12 Airline Resolutions

I f there is a business in need of change, it is the airline business. So as you ponder your resolutions for next year, here are a few thoughts on what the airline industry ought to consider. They're the result of an informal poll of passengers I took last year.

1. **Fly in our shoes.** Airline chief executives and top management need to know what it is really like to be a passenger. I don't mean flying in First Class, nonstop. I mean the very back of Economy Class, Friday night, connecting through Chicago O'Hare or JFK in the peak of winter or summer. No special treatment. They could grasp the real experience of flying on their airline. It astounds me that in this day and time, the top brass are making decisions when they have no clue on the reality of the situation.

2. **Love the one you're with.** If you are content with your current airline of choice, stick with it. Don't change your whole itinerary because Sam's Airline is $40 cheaper. In the end, you will have a smoother experience with an airline you can rely on. This sends a message to other airlines on what is really important.

3. **Like it — or leave it.** Attention, airline employees! If you don't like your job, start looking or preparing for a different one, because it isn't going to get any better for the foreseeable future. There are too many attendants with bad attitudes out there and, warranted or not, the passenger does pay your salary. They are not the cause for your frustration. As my mother-in-law said to me, "Maybe it is time to give up this Peter Pan lifestyle if you don't see the magic in it." And before you blast me for this one, yes, I may take my own advice.

4. **Keep it in the U.S.** There has to be a limit on the outsourcing that is taking place. The airlines are outsourcing Americans out of too many jobs. Do you know that the airline you fly with is probably planning on moving 35 percent of its mechanics' slots outside the country? This is not a case for when your TV breaks down because of being assembled in Mexico; this is your loved ones' life and livelihood on the line.

5. **Enough of the false advertising.** How many times do you choose an airline because of an amenity that it promised, only to find out that the small print states that it is only allowed on every third Wednesday of every fourth month of the year? The airlines have to be held accountable for misleading the public.

6. **Re-regulate.** It has become quite evident that airlines are not in control of their financial faculties and most are in bankruptcy protection. They are cutting everything except the actual flying part and yet continue to commit financial suicide. If there was a fare cap, high and low, maybe the airlines would focus on performance, safety, and, yes, even service.

7. **Face reality.** Passengers have to realize that airline service is not what it used to be. The Pan Am's ice molds or TWA's caviar servings are things of the past. Those airlines are gone and the current

ones are in it to make money, not to employ, enrich or to please. It has been proven that passengers are mostly interested in cheaper fares, so they must share some of the blame for the service downfall.

8. **Be safe and secure.** There has to be more tolerance for airline security and the TSA. Yes, I get frustrated by the long lines, the inconsistencies, and the invasions of my personal privacy, but what we easily overlook are the daily responsibilities of these people. Can you imagine going to work each day and preventing a terrorist from bringing down a flight? I confront security approximately five times a week, and I don't like it better than you, but at least I have a safer feeling knowing everyone is scrutinized in the same manner.

9. **Lead parachutes.** A company in bankruptcy is a company in trouble, period. It can't control its finances and needs help from the court system to hold off the creditors. Why are the bankruptcy judges allowing massive pay cuts for the workers but bonuses and golden parachutes for the top brass? It makes no sense to me, but it has to stop.

10. **Reform pensions.** While many airline employees lose their pensions, the average passenger doesn't know why that should concern them. Two reasons: First, pensions are guaranteed by a government agency that takes over when an airline is forced into a financial corner. So, in a sense, the airline is dumping the cost of the pensions of its employees on the federal government, which is paid by your taxes. Second, don't think it will stop with the airlines. This form of cutthroat business usually has a domino effect and before long it will leak into the corporate world and gone is that nest egg you are relying upon.

11. **Right hand, meet left hand.** Communication is the key to any successful business. Management has to listen to its frontline employees and passengers. From connecting flights and wheelchairs, to cost cutting and customer satisfaction issues, nobody is listening. I have had a simple suggestion on file with my airline for over four years now. It would save an average of $1,100 a flight and

increase customer satisfaction tremendously. I don't want money or recognition for the idea, I just want to help. My airline is too big and can't listen, so I watch the problem repeat itself flight after flight. I even wrote to my chief executive. He hasn't gotten back to me as of yet.

12. **Prepare for life in the zoo.** Airline employers can keep cutting paychecks, work rules, and pensions, but when their current employees get fed up and leave, they will find that when you pay peanuts, you only get monkeys.

CHAPTER TWO

Warning: Bumpy Summer Ahead

L ast year, I predicted a bumpy summer for air travel. Sure enough, the season experienced a record number of cancellations and a lower customer satisfaction rating, but overall, the airline industry did better than I expected. I think that's because so many airlines were in such dire financial difficulty that the employees were in last-ditch survival mode.

Will we get the same lift this year? Don't count on it. What's different from last year?

1. **Going mad**. Most airline employees are angry that their paychecks and pensions have been slashed while the CEOs are raking in record salaries and stock options. It seems that sacrifices have not been shared by top management, and that doesn't sit well with the frontline employees.

2. **Understaffed.** Many airlines are short on employees, and have been for some time, but this year they are especially short on pilots. A flight can operate—poorly—with a shortage of flight attendants, gate agents and mechanics, but there is no flying at all without a full complement up front. The airlines are counting on pilots to pick up extra hours to make up for the summer load. Let's see . . . less money, no pension, CEO making a record salary? Can you read the tea leaves here? My prediction is that many flights will cancel because of this pilot shortage.

3. **Overcrowded skies.** Now that the airline industry is beginning to bounce back, many airlines are adding new routes. New routes mean more traffic, and more traffic means more delays and cancellations. New flights also call for the hiring of more employees, something management seems not to understand.

4. **Sold out.** Airlines are already selling out flights for the summer. This is great for the industry's per-seat revenue numbers, but what happens when a flight cancels? You can't put the passengers on the next flight when there are no seats available. Sold-out flights create a domino effect, which leaves many passengers fuming by the end of the day.

As a flight attendant, I dread the summer flying season. The hot, sweaty, manic, busy lines, plus the oversold flights, packed check-in counters, flight delays, cancellations, manpower shortages, and unhappy passengers all add up to one big nightmare. I would give anything to have June and August off.

If I am gun-shy as this season approaches, it's because I think of the summer of 2000, which was the worst summer travel season I have ever experienced. That year, work slowdowns and flight cancellations caused a giant customer-service fiasco. I was yelled at so many times that I started wearing an overcoat in the terminal to disguise the fact that I worked for an airline.

So, what can you do to ensure an easier summer flight? I've been a flight attendant for 18 summer seasons, and I offer you my "Top 10 Summer Flying Tips":

1. **Skycap.** Instead of waiting three hours to check in a bag, give it to the skycap. It may cost you a couple of bucks per bag but believe me, halfway through the check-in line you will wish you had.

2. **Electronic check-in.** Some flights are eligible for online check-in. By avoiding the check-in mess, you can go directly to the security mess.

3. **Early bird.** Take an early flight. As the day progresses, there is a greater likelihood of flight cancellations and weather delays.

4. **Bring a jacket.** Some of the coldest flights I have ever flown have been in the summer, when the pilots overcompensate for the heat by cranking up the air conditioning to Siberian levels.

5. **Don't stop.** Pay the extra money and book the nonstop flight if available. You may get a good deal by connecting through Chicago, but believe me you will pay for it later.

6. **Be prepared.** Don't have something crucial planned for the first two days of your trip. For example, if your cruise leaves on Friday morning, don't leave Thursday night.

7. **Make the call.** Call the airline before you leave for the airport to make sure your flight is on time. Sign up for e-check, a service many airlines provide; it will call your cell phone to inform you of any delays. If you are being picked up at your destination, make sure your driver has a number to call to verify your arrival time.

8. **Do unto others.** Treat other travelers and airline employees as you would like to be treated yourself. Put yourself in their shoes and realize that you are not the only person in this world.

9. **Stick to the favorites.** If you have had better experiences on one airline than on others, stick with it, even if it is a little more expensive or leaves at a less convenient time. Your judgment is key.

10. **Pack a lot of patience.** Don't let small inconveniences ruin the whole trip. Things go wrong in life and your airplane trip may be no different.

Oh yeah, one more thing: I know my summer prediction is a bit gloomy, but try to have fun. Isn't that why you travel in the summer in the first place?

Happy summer flying. Maybe I will be on-board with some of you. I will be the one with the goofy smile wearing the polyester suit and the tie that matches the curtains.

CHAPTER THREE

10 Tips for Surviving an Airline Strike

The process of airline labor negotiations is the biggest chess game in the business world today. What the company is willing to give and what the workers are demanding are most assuredly different. When sides disagree, you're at an impasse. And here's where the tactics get tricky. The newest airline trend is to declare bankruptcy and have the judge help the company do away with the workers' contracts. My question is, what judge in this land would cut a workforce's pension but not touch the upper management's multi-million dollar pensions? Am I missing something here?

I have not yet taken part in a full-out strike, but I am sure one is in my future. I listen to the employees who have, and their civil war accounts are both fascinating and frightening. The employees who work for my airline carry around a little "scab" book. A scab is anyone who ever crossed a picket line or disregarded a planned work stoppage.

If a scab is on their crew, the other crewmembers are alerted and give them the silent treatment for the duration of the flight, like kids shunning another child on a playground. The result of course, is that the atmosphere up-front is always strained. The father of an old friend of mine was a former scab. When my friend joined his father's airline as a pilot, he changed his last name so he couldn't be associated with his dad's previous actions. It sounds quite childish, but such treatment is very effective.

If you are a scheduled passenger on an airline that is experiencing labor problems with threats of a strike looming in the background, there are precautionary measures you should keep in mind. Here are some tips for flying through airline work actions:

1. **Double book.** Make a back-up reservation on a different airline. You can always cancel and get a refund, but the closer it gets to the date, the higher the price, with fewer alternatives available.

2. **Give yourself credit.** Pay for your ticket with a credit card and study up on its charge-back policies.

3. **Listen up.** Pay attention to media sources and timelines. If you are flying within a week of possible work stoppages, then prepare back-up plans and alternate routing.

4. **Money back guarantee?** Make sure you read the refund policy on the ticket you purchased. Many Internet tickets are cheap but are non-refundable, period.

5. **Skip the line.** If you are at the airport when a work action takes place, it will undoubtedly cause a commotion. Call reservations as quickly as you can. Have that number readily available along with a few numbers from other airlines.

6. **Proof of flight.** When booking a flight, get a paper ticket. Ticketless travel, or e-tickets, are usually non-endorsable on other airlines.

7. **Get informed.** During these times, unions provide recorded messages that relay specific information on issues and dates. You may or may not care about the issues but the dates are important.

8. **Carry-on but pack light.** You will almost never hear a flight attendant recommend carry-on luggage but in these circumstances I do. Switching flights can be less of a hassle without checked luggage. Remember, you can always gate-check your bag.

9. **On the house.** Ask for vouchers for food, hotel, and phone calls. Remember that the airline is responsible for reimbursing costs that are not weather-related.

10. **Check your mental baggage.** The people at whom you yell may be the same individuals who would have helped you.

While all airlines go through this at times, the airlines to patronize are those that deal most effectively with labor problems. Some say that if employees go on strike and drive the airline out of business, it may solve the overcapacity issue plaguing the industry these days. While this is not necessarily true, it does mean a sharp increase in your ticket price.

What do the specific issues have to do with you, the passenger? When airlines start cutting pensions, it tends to have a trickle-down effect. Be careful, because your own pension could be targeted next.

CHAPTER FOUR

Airline Complaint? Well, Speak Up!

I have read several reports recently stating that airline complaints are decreasing. Are the airlines getting better at what they do, or are people just giving up? I mean, have you ever tried to figure out where to file a complaint? Sure, there may be an address in the in-flight magazine, sandwiched somewhere between the boring editorials and the ads for crappy gifts, but who takes those magazines home? I wonder how many people get steamed, write a letter, and then throw it away because they don't know where to send it.

As a flight attendant, you might not expect me to encourage complaints against airlines, but I do. I am even going to give you some effective techniques for complaining, along with a list of addresses. Why? Because the airlines are losing touch with their employees. Union concerns, greed, and distrust are rampant after all the bankruptcies, contract renegotiations, and pension cuts. Airline executives will no longer listen to their frontline workers, so it is up to the customers to speak up and be heard.

But before you compose your letter of complaint, you must compose yourself. Here are some tips for effective complaining:

1. **Be reasonable.** Count to 10, put the shoe on the other foot, and consider whether your grievance is worth making a big fuss about. If it's just a bruised ego or a misunderstanding, then let it go. Save the big guns for the real trouble.

2. **Report rudeness.** Despite what I just said, always report outright rudeness. An employee who is overly rude is probably a repeat offender. Enough complaint letters against that person will bring results.

3. **Get the details.** As soon as the incident occurs, write down as much information as you can. Names, date and time, flight numbers, baggage carousel numbers—anything you remember that can help you accurately describe the event in question.

4. **Get a witness.** If you are treated very badly and a neutral party sees it happen, get his or her name and number. Witness testimony carries a lot of weight when it comes to resolving a grievance.

5. **Try for immediate resolution.** If you have the time and the patience, try to get the problem fixed immediately. That's your best shot at a satisfactory resolution. As time goes, the complaint loses its urgency for everyone involved.

6. **Keep your temper.** You might be furious, but yelling at me at the top of your lungs in-flight is just wasted energy. Maybe I'll agree with you, or maybe I'll nod to placate you, or maybe I'll just notice you have bad breath. In any case, yelling won't improve your chances of a positive outcome, and it could get you in trouble. You don't want to appear to threaten a flight attendant; that's a violation of FAA rules.

7. **Write a letter.** If immediate resolution is not possible, the best chance of a satisfactory outcome is by writing a letter or e-mail.

8. **Know the rules.** The purchase of a ticket makes a contract between you and the airline. You have certain rights, but the airline is not responsible for everything that can go awry. For example: The airline is required to get you to your final destination, but if weather causes a delay, you might find yourself out of pocket for a hotel stay; because the delay is not the airline's fault, it is not liable for your costs. So before you complain, read the fine print.

9. **Just the facts, ma'am.** You don't want to write a letter that starts out, "Dear CEO, Your airline is crap." While that may be true, the tone will produce very few good results.

10. **Know what you want.** Whether it be an apology, change of procedure, someone's job or compensation, be specific about what action from the airline will satisfy you.

11. **Don't expect too much.** Be reasonable with your demands. In fact, it may be best to expect nothing. That way, you will be pleasantly surprised if you get a reply, and if you don't, at least you will have the satisfaction of having spoken your mind.

12. **If all else fails, change airlines.** If you don't get the response you had hoped for or you are dissatisfied with the result, then change airlines. Having to suffer through flight after flight with an airline that you have come to hate will turn you into a sourpuss, and that's bad for your mental health.

Passenger complaints can be very helpful to frontline employees, especially complaints about insufficient staffing or workers who look wracked by flu and seem like they should be in bed. Such complaints send a distinct message to management to stop overworking that one gate agent and punishing flight attendants who call in sick.

On the other side of the coin are compliments. You know, praise for that certain someone who saved your flight from being a total disaster. Just as the rude ones deserve reprimand, so do the helpful ones deserve commendation. I know they are getting harder and harder to find, but they are out there and they need an occasional pat on the back.

I once received a commendation letter remarking how funny I was and making particular mention of my ability to poke fun at airline idiocy. Sadly, it was taken as a letter of complaint and counted as a black mark in my personnel file. But it's the thought that counts.

If your complaint is safety related, you need to address your concern to the Federal Aviation Administration (FAA) at:

Assistant Administrator for System Safety ASY-100
Federal Aviation Administration
800 Independence Ave., S.W.
Washington, D.C. 20591

You can also contact the FAA by phone at 800-FAA-SURE (800-322-7873). If it has to do with security, it should go to the Transportation Security Administration (TSA) by phone at the TSA Contact Center (866-289-9673) or by e-mail at tsa-contactcenter@dhs.gov.

If your complaint is airline-specific, you can go to the airline's website and look under customer relations. You can use those links for the compliments as well.

And always try to remember, the frontline workers don't write the lyrics, they just sing the song!

CHAPTER FIVE

No, and I'm Sorry

N o. Nein. Nix. Nyet. Nope. Nuh-unh. No way. Not gonna happen.

"No: An interjection used to indicate a negative response in order to refuse, deny or disagree with something."

There should be a cross-reference: "See Airline."

Many years ago, an airline ad said, "Our stewardesses never say 'No'. Well, almost never." And not so long ago, when I went through training for my first job as a flight attendant, we were told that the word "No" should be removed from our vocabulary. This instruction would bring on the usual promiscuity jokes, but it was reinforced throughout our training. There was always a way around that abrupt refusal to help: responses like "I will see what I can do" and "How about … instead" or "Let me check on that."

Sadly, this tradition of willing service and gentle dissembling has disappeared from the no-longer-so-friendly skies. In fact, considering the financial mess most airlines are facing, I'm surprised they haven't rented out the back of employee uniforms to advertisers. Actually, some airlines do put badges on their flight attendants saying chipper things like "We love to fly" and "We are going places." With all the cutbacks taking place, these flight attendants should just slap a neon badge on their chests with a big, fat "No!" emblazoned on it. I would wear it—that way I could just point to the badge and answer 90 percent of passengers' questions without ever opening my mouth.

Is there a meal on today's flight?

No.

Can I have the whole can?

No.

Any pillows or blankets on-board?

No.

Are there going to be any empty seats on today's flight?

No.

Do airline employees have a pension?

No! (Had to get that one in.)

Do you respect your airline?

Uh, let me guess … No?

Well, you get the picture. Most days, I feel like the guy on the Capitol One commercial on TV, except I'm not having that much fun. And, I'm willing to bet, neither are you. Let me ask you some questions.

Is your seat comfortable?

No.

Did you make your connecting flight?

No.

Is it your fault that so many airlines are in financial distress?

No.

Do you like your flight attendant?

No, sorry, not very much.

And no wonder! We tell you what you can't do, shout at you when you are up and the "Fasten seat belt" sign is on, and say "No" at least a hundred times a flight. We put on our insult-proof faces, but after full loads and multiple paycuts, our bad attitudes are beginning to show.

Of course, some passengers won't take "No" for an answer. They are usually lawyers or psychologists of some kind, people who think they can argue it up enough to get a "Yes."

Can I have a pillow?

No.

Why not?

Because we don't have any left.

And why is that?

Because the airline is cutting back.

But I had a pillow on a different airline.

Then why are you here?

So, what you're saying is that I should fly with that other airline?

Yes.

See? In the end, he did get a "Yes."

As airline management keeps rewarding itself with big bonuses and stock options, I feel very little remorse about saying "No" at the drop of a hat.

Speaking of remorse, here is another phrase that needs reviewing: "I'm sorry."

When I flew for Pan Am, I used to say I was sorry about 50 times a flight. (Toward the end of Pan Am's existence, I thought its motto should be changed to "I'm sorry.") I don't say "I'm sorry" anymore because heartfelt apologies weigh you down too much. I can't and no longer will apologize for something that is out of my control.

Many people ask me if I see airline service getting better anytime soon. I look at all the airlines in bankruptcy proceedings and at the rancor that has taken hold in the industry, and once again answer, "No."

And for that I am sorry.

Here's Looking at You

J etBlue's emergency landing at LAX grabbed headlines all over the
world. Like most onlookers, I was impressed by two things: the
heroic and nearly flawless response of the crew (both pilots and
flight attendants), and the weirdness of the media event.

As we all know by now, the passengers on the disabled aircraft were
able to watch live television coverage of their own emergency up until 10 minutes before landing. As a flight attendant myself, I think I
would have shut off the system immediately. Before you disagree with
me, read the entire chapter; if you still disagree with me, send me an
e-mail.

My main objection is that the in-flight coverage could have led to
panic or distracted the passengers from hearing the crew's instructions.
Believe me, in an emergency you really need everyone's full attention.

But camera trouble is nothing new in the airline industry. There once was a system that allowed passengers to watch the goings-on in the cockpit (at the pilots' discretion, of course). One airline was known for showing a live shot of the flight panels and instruments during takeoffs and landings. On one flight, a pilot decided to get cute and put a banana in the middle of the shot.

When it was time to pull up the landing gear, the pilot donned a gorilla arm he'd gotten at a costume shop; the next thing the passengers saw was a hairy arm retract the gear and grab the banana. Minutes later the peel was tossed away in plain sight. All the passengers thought it was hilarious, except for one. That person prevailed in a costly lawsuit, shutting down the camera on that airline for good.

On a different airline, the cockpit camera was once turned on accidentally in-flight. It was pointed directly at the captain. While the copilot was off on a restroom break, the passengers got a full shot of the captain's extended nose-mining experience. The passengers laughed till they cried.

Another airline unplugged its cockpit cameras after one of its airplanes crashed in Chicago, killing all aboard. A relative of one of the passengers filed a lawsuit and won a monumental settlement, claiming undue pain and suffering on behalf of the passengers who witnessed their imminent demise live on camera.

That's what surprised me most about the JetBlue incident. The "banana peel" plaintiff prevailed on the basis of 10 seconds of terror caught on tape. What would have happened if the JetBlue emergency had ended badly, after 40 minutes of live television coverage?

Of course, Big Brother is still alive and well elsewhere in the airline industry. In fact, in a typical day of flying the average passenger will be watched from a surveillance device at least 10 times.

1. In the airport parking lot

2. At curbside check-in

3. At the flight check-in area

4. In the security line

5. During the security screening process

6. In the post-security area

7. In the terminal

8. At the gate

9. At the arrival destination

10. At passport control (on an international flight) or in the baggage claim area (on a domestic flight)

Now some airlines are introducing an onboard surveillance system to keep an eye on the cabin in-flight. Flight crews are fighting the move, fearing supervisors may later scrutinize the tapes. So far, onboard surveillance has prevented a man from choking while waiting for the lavatory, caught a few thieves stealing alcohol miniatures, and discovered a couple pulling a Monica Lewinsky in the back galley when the flight attendants were busy elsewhere.

As of yet, there are no cameras in the restrooms (at least, not so far as we know). But where will it all end? Are we safer for the cameras' presence, or is it 1984 after all?

Certainly there are good arguments for increased camera presence. Video surveillance has been proven to reduce general crime by as much as 90 percent. Perhaps it could do the same at airports. And I have to admit, I feel more comfortable with video surveillance now than I did when I was younger and had more to hide.

But what do you think? Should JetBlue have shut off the TV? Should some of those cameras be yanked from the airport? And what about cameras in the cabin? Is privacy the price of security?

CHAPTER SEVEN

You're Fired! Top Airline Dismissals

F ired, laid off, let go, asked to resign, made redundant, got the ax—
whatever you want to call it, it's time to take a number at the unemployment office. But where do you go, exactly, if you have been
a pilot, flight attendant, or gate agent for 20 years and know nothing
else? Wall Street? Wal-Mart? No, most airline employees just line up
at the next airline hiring—unless, of course, they were fired for some
ridiculously outrageous conduct.

Here are some bizarre examples from the file.

1. On a trans-Atlantic flight, a mother of a 19-month-old toddler
became suspicious when she spotted powdery specks floating in
her screaming baby's juice. It turned out to be a sedative called
Xanax, which had been added to the juice by a flight attendant.

Apparently, he was trying to calm the baby and make it a better flight for the other passengers. Needless to say, he was fired and charges were brought against him.

2. A flight attendant on the way to work phoned in a bomb threat for the flight he was scheduled to work, with the idea of getting the flight canceled so he could attend a party. What is even more idiotic is this: After he got cut off on the first attempt, he called back. He was arrested in the airport parking lot.

3. A male flight attendant was at his boiling point and decided to teach an annoying passenger a lesson. Under his breath he whispered to the passenger, "If you don't shut up for the remainder of the flight, I am going to kick your ass off this plane and claim you threatened me first." The passenger was on the airline's board of directors.

4. Two pilots playing a joke on one of the flight attendants took their clothes off in-flight and called the flight attendant up to the cockpit. The wrong flight attendant came up and, let's just say, did not have the anticipated sense of humor.

5. A gate agent was dealing with an irate passenger who proceeded to insult his mother. It was the last straw, and they came to blows. The gate agent won, as he broke the customer's nose and two ribs, but found himself out of a job.

6. On a layover happy hour, a pilot tried to slip a date-rape drug into the drink of one of his flight attendants, but missed and put it into his own drink instead. After noticing the pilot behaving strangely, an off-duty police officer, who had witnessed the whole event, called for backup and took the pilot away for questioning. Later the police discovered over 200 tablets of the sedative in his room.

7. A flight attendant couldn't get off work for her 10K race, so she called in sick and ran the race anyway. She won third place in her age division. Unfortunately, the woman she edged out for the prize was her sick-leave supervisor.

8. A flight attendant was in the crowd at David Letterman's show. When the host came out for an audience skit, he interviewed her. She must have been addled by the spotlight because when she announced what she did for a living and what airline she worked for, she added that her company didn't like people. Even David Letterman winced. Among the millions of viewers that night was the airline's CEO, who personally fired her himself.

9. A male flight attendant who worked with me at Pan Am had a bizarre sense of humor. He was known as "The Gasser" because he found it exciting to air his malady in awkward and enclosed environments like cockpits, buses, and galleys. I thought the guy was interesting but one of the strangest characters I had ever met. He eventually got fired after he let loose in an airport elevator with the CFO on-board. After further analysis of his record, he was given a psychiatric dismissal. In this case, to air was not human.

10. A pilot known as "Don Juan" for his multiple sexual encounters was finally fired for having sex with his chief pilot's wife. The pilot was on a restroom break with the lady when they were discovered by the husband. How exactly do you explain the situation when the door opens? "This is not what it looks like"?

11. A reservations agent was hoping to fly standby to Hawaii for vacation, but he found all the flights were full. Knowing the computer system pretty well, he booked a whole First Class cabin under a fake oil tycoon's name. He and his wife got First Class seats on that flight to Hawaii, but an unemployment notice was waiting for him when he got home.

12. A flight attendant was asked by a popular men's magazine to pose naked for one of their pictorials. Not wanting to lose her job, she consulted with her union. Apparently, she misunderstood the regulations because she posed in—and out—of her airline uniform, mentioned her airline by name several times, and even added a personal picture of her next to a plane with the airline's logo in plain sight. She was totally surprised that she was fired and couldn't imagine why.

13. On a flight from Dallas, a flight attendant produced a note that read, "There is a bomb on-board. Long live Saddam." The flight attendant eventually admitted that she had written the note herself, but didn't say why.

14. Two flight attendants on a Russian airliner attacked a passenger for accusing them of being drunk. An alcohol test proved that the flight attendants were indeed intoxicated. What? That's not allowed in Russia?

15. A flight attendant of 25 years developed a nervous twitch after a mechanical mishap affected the wiring for a flight's call system. Apparently, the call bell went off every three seconds for the whole 12-hour flight. After that incident, every time she heard the sound, she would repeat, *"Bing, bing, bing"* every three seconds until she reached the passenger and turned off the call button. Her peers found it humorous at first but became worried when she couldn't stop. She eventually got a permanent psychiatric leave of absence, proving that pinging bells can be hazardous to your health.

CHAPTER EIGHT

10 Wacky Airline Lawsuits

A s a flight attendant for a major airline, I've attended countless classes on cultural awareness, sexual harassment, and passenger diversity. I've been told how to talk, where not to put my hands—even when to laugh and when to shut up. All of this comes with an increasing fear of lawsuits. And small wonder: These days, airlines often settle lawsuits, even when the plaintiff's case is weak, just to avoid bad publicity and lawyers' fees. Of course, this practice opens the floodgates to some pretty interesting lawsuits. Here is my collection of the Top 10 Wacko Airline Lawsuits:

1. **Pink Foul.** In 1995, a 24-year-old male filed a lawsuit against a major international airline for not hiring him as a flight attendant because he was homosexual. First of all, how would they know his

sexual preference? I don't think there is a check-off box for that on the application. And second, call me crazy, but isn't "flight attendant" one of the most popular careers for gay men?

2. **What's the Buzz?** A middle-aged woman filed a lawsuit against Delta Air Lines for public humiliation after a Delta security agent approached her on the plane before takeoff and informed her that something in her checked bag was vibrating. She was then escorted off the plane in full sight of onlookers to identify the suspect device, which she told the agent was probably an adult toy that she had picked up on her trip. Not satisfied with her answer, the agent instructed the woman to hold the device up and turn it on. When she did, the security agent allegedly began to "laugh hysterically." Embarrassed or not, the passenger got the names of more than 10 witnesses for her case.

3. **Plop Plop, Fizz Fizz.** Now that airlines are doing away with their complimentary food service, the quality of the food has certainly gotten better. But two years ago, a businessman filed a lawsuit against an airline saying his meal was so bad that he blew a multi-million-dollar account. Why? Because during his meeting he was running to the bathroom every few minutes. I don't know how he could prove the airline food was at fault, but I've become violently ill from airline food once or twice in my 15 years with the airlines, and it's not pretty. Believe me, there's nothing worse than being stuck in one of those airplane lavatories for hours on end.

4. **Cut the Fat.** A lawyer from Ohio filed a lawsuit against Delta Air Lines claiming that he suffered "embarrassment, severe discomfort, mental anguish and severe emotional distress" from having to sit next to a passenger so overweight that they were "figuratively married from the right kneecap to the shoulder" for the duration of the flight. The plaintiff alleged that the airline breached its contract to provide him with a full seat. He was seeking unspecified damages but was open to a settlement. Sounds like somebody wanted a free upgrade.

5. **Everybody's a Comedian.** Southwest Airlines is known for its humorous announcements and antics, but when the humor is taken

as prejudice, lawsuits tend to fly. A flight attendant made the following announcement to get everyone seated before departure: "Eenie, meenie, minie, moe. Pick a seat, 'cause it's time to go." At the time, there were only two women still standing, both African-Americans, and they took offense at the use of the nursery rhyme, which once had quite different wording.

6. **What a Dope.** A passenger who was traveling from Hawaii to California was arrested as he retrieved his bag, which contained over a pound of marijuana. The passenger filed a lawsuit against the airline claiming that a baggage handler must have planted the drugs in his bag. Now, I've heard of people accusing airline workers of stealing things from their bags, but this is the first I've heard of them leaving a present.

7. **Got milk?** A female pilot filed a lawsuit against her airline when she was terminated for using a breast pump. Now, I have to tread lightly here as my wife is a pilot and a new mom. The airline defended its action, saying it did not object to the pilot using a breast pump in principle, but did object when she was simultaneously flying the airplane. In the pilot's defense, I must say that the airlines don't usually provide adequate leaves of absence or proper work breaks, so the working pilot is forced to pump when she can. My wife included.

8. **C-E-Uh-Oh.** An airline CEO filed a lawsuit against his own liquidated airline for failure to provide full compensation. The exec received his millions, his golf club membership, and full health insurance, but he was not able to collect on his free lifetime First Class flights. Aw, now doesn't that just break your heart? Thousands of employees lost their pensions, and this guy is crying because he now has to pay for his air travel. One question, sir: If the airline has liquidated, where do you think your settlement will come from?

9. **Fling.** A female passenger caught her husband in the lavatory with another woman, then filed a lawsuit against the airline because the pilot had made an announcement making suggestive reference to the "Mile High Club." Let me get this straight: It's not

the husband's fault; it's the airline's fault? Where was that reasoning when Bill Clinton needed it?

10. **Flung.** The CFO of a prominent company was upset that he didn't get an upgrade to First Class on his international flight. He then got drunk and belligerent, defecated on the serving cart, and smeared feces onto the cabin walls. The airline won a suit requiring him to refund every passenger's full-fare First Class ticket. When the defendant filed a countersuit saying it was the airline's fault for serving him too much alcohol, the case was thrown out of court. Can you imagine waking up from that hangover? *"I did what?"*

Some class-action lawsuits have been good for the airline industry, especially the one filed on behalf of flight attendants against the tobacco and airline industries in a case claiming harm from secondhand smoke. Result: No more smoking on the airplane.

When you hear of a ridiculous lawsuit victory, it's OK to laugh. But don't cheer too hard for a multimillion-dollar judgment, because at the end of the day, the costly settlement will show up in your ticket price. Ah, lawyers, the necessary evil: You can't live with them, and you can't settle without them.

CHAPTER NINE

Just Fooling Around

Tant here is nothing like a little practical joke in the workplace to brighten up the day. It just so happens that my workplace is at 35,000 feet and while safety is the number one concern, we all need a release from time to time.

Occasionally we have the right crew and circumstances to let loose. There are milder ones like sticking "CREW USE ONLY" on the back of a cute flight attendant, or rolling the butterballs in coffee grounds and serving them to the cockpit as chocolate truffles. We make instant dribble glasses by piercing holes in the plastic containers, or chill the coffee so that when the passenger says that the coffee is ice cold, you know that this time they weren't exaggerating.

After exhausting the run of mild pranks, we tend to move onto the more intricate ones, like putting coffee grounds on top of a crewmember's suitcase, so when he retrieves it at the end of a flight, he gets a dry coffee shower.

There is nothing quite like the satisfaction of a successful, well-planned prank. For example, a while back I placed a small cup of dry lemonade powder above my fellow joker's seat. When the plane landed and the brakes pulled the airplane's momentum forward, the cup tipped over, and doused his black hair with golden powder.

He laughed for a second, and then headed straight for the nearest toilet. Where, incidentally, a large cup of water had been carefully propped up on top of the door waiting for him. It drenched him as he entered, causing the powder to harden along with his hair. On his next five flights, he got me back by announcing my cell phone number as the new air travel help line.

I received over 200 phone calls and a big monthly bill.

Sometimes we play pranks on overly abusive passengers. They are usually mild, like changing the combination on a suitcase, or giving out First Class carnations, knowing full well that they would be sent to agricultural inspection when completing customs in the United States. We would feel that small sense of payback as we passed them being searched in the agricultural section.

Speaking of rude passengers, why would anyone who's being overly rude to a flight attendant ask them for airport directions? It has happened to me many times and while I have usually resisted the impulse, twice I have sent them on a wild goose chase.

Sometimes pranks in-flight can get a bit out of hand. I heard about a couple of pilots wanting to have fun with a brand new flight attendant. They told her that there was a problem with the landing gear. She was instructed to go out to the middle section of the cabin and jump up and down a couple of times in hopes of dislodging it. It was hilarious at the time, but one of the pilots eventually got suspended for it.

One joke even got a couple of pilots fired. The captain's girlfriend was working up front so the pilots decided to pull their greatest prank by completely disrobing in-flight and requesting their crew meal. Unfortunately, by the time their meal was ready, the girlfriend had gone to the back. Let's just say that her replacement did not have the same sense of humor.

When the safety demonstration is not on video, many jokes can be played. For example, writing something funny in the inside of a safety card like "I am sexually frustrated." Rarely does the flight attendant look inside before unfolding it to show the passengers. My favorite was to insert a live air cartridge in the demo life vest—when the flight attendant pulls down the handle during the demonstration, the vest inflates and delivers quite a surprise. I can remember a young flight attendant actually wetting her pants on that one.

Do you ever wonder why flight attendants occasionally break out in laughter during the safety demonstration? No, we don't consider the demo a particularly funny thing to watch either. What you don't realize is that as you sit watching the flight attendant up front, she can see her colleagues standing in the back of the cabin, who are probably acting in some obscene or moronic manner to get her to laugh.

They are playing a game of "Gotcha." The flight attendant facing you wins if she can keep a straight face. A smile is considered a draw, and a laugh or leaving the demo position is a loss. If she doesn't look, then it's considered chickening out, and not very sporting.

Yes, you might call it juvenile or even silly, but it passes the time and it makes for a much-needed laugh. I can't see the harm in it all as long as it doesn't infringe on personal safety.

Laughter is one of the most precious things in this world, and life should not be taken so seriously, especially in these stressful times.

CHAPTER TEN

What a Waste

We are fortunate to live in a time of plenty and in a country where starvation is rare. Our food production is at such levels that wastage is normal, and two-thirds of all Americans are deemed overweight. Our government subsidizes farmers to produce surpluses that are often plowed under, and the cycle of waste continues from store to consumer.

There is waste in the airline industry, too. The amount of trash and discarded food that accumulates is staggering. Yes, though it seems the airlines are not feeding you much, they waste as much as they use. The opportunities for recycling are mind-boggling.

Companies claim recycling costs too much. If this is the case, then lawmakers should issue tax incentives for recycling. Make it uneconomical to waste-and-toss, and companies will be setting up recycling bins in every corner of the workplace.

As for the airlines, they should initiate programs that will encourage employees not to open consumables until necessary, reuse whatever they can, and take steps toward recycling. I know most flight attendants would be more than happy to comply. Everyone understands that the landfills are full and that our children will inherit our mess.

Only now, when wastage is hitting them in their already-sore bank accounts, are the airlines starting programs to minimize waste. Here are the only two conservation measures that I have personally witnessed, along with some comments about how they will affect passengers.

1. **No water until pushback.** Pilots are now under strict instructions to keep the water shut off until the plane leaves the gate. It is estimated that this policy will save up to $500 each trip. The only drawback is if you go to the restroom while still at the gate: The toilet may work, but you won't be able to wash your hands afterward. I guess the pilots have a clause about coffee, however, because when they find out they can't get their java right away, water mysteriously appears.

2. **Engine shutdowns.** Engines are being shut down more often these days as a fuel-saving measure, so you may find yourself parked on a remote taxiway with the engines shut off during a weather delay. Prepare yourself for a lengthy wait, and know your rights should you want to get off the airplane. Every airline has its own rules, so you will need to do some research about this in advance of your flight.

These two "conservation" measures are really cost-saving measures. I am more concerned about world resources than about company profits. Here, then, are some other conservation measures that I think should be standard operating procedures for all airlines.

1. Recycle aluminum cans as well as discarded newspapers and magazines left aboard the aircraft.

2. Donate unused, shelf-stable foods such as cereal and crackers to food banks for the poor.

3. Use only one engine to taxi.

4. Lower cruising speeds.

5. Use flight simulators rather than real aircraft for pilot training.

6. Serve food on ceramic dishes (rather than plastic and paper) aboard aircraft.

7. Reclaim glycol, the fluid used to de-ice aircraft, for reuse as a runway de-icer or as antifreeze for automobiles.

8. When appropriate, hold aircraft at gates, with the engines shut down, when weather or other problems delay takeoff.

Here are some things that passengers can do to help:

1. **Ask about conservation, and support those airlines that are making a big effort.** Many airlines claim to be environmentally friendly and say they engage in recycling programs. What they don't tell you is that they purchase recycled products but don't complete the recycling triangle by recycling them after they've used them. Instead, they throw them away. Ask your flight attendant whether the airline recycles. If she doesn't know, chances are it doesn't.

2. **Keep your cup.** If you are a frequent beverage consumer onboard, hold on to your plastic cup for refills. It may be a small thing, but it's a start.

3. **Look around.** Notice how things get wasted at airports and in-flight. (Why do I see many recycling containers in European airports, but very few in the States?) Write letters with suggestions. If you threaten to take your business elsewhere, the airline brass may take notice.

Recently, during a long airport delay between flights, I realized that modern airport technology can also be energy-saving. As I walked around the new high-tech airport, I observed technology at its finest—everything from moving walkways to Internet kiosks.

The doors opened automatically as I walked into the restroom. The urinal had a sensor and flushed for me. When I washed my hands, the water turned on and off by itself, as did the hand dryer. Besides ensuring sanitation and ease of use, these innovations save a lot of water and electricity. In the past, open taps and paper towels added up to millions of dollars. The more I looked around me, the more evidence I found of good conservation practice through modern technology. That is a sign for hope.

I left the airport restroom through the automatic doors, having touched nothing through the entire process—well, almost nothing. But if modern technology ever gets to the level of the automatic zipper-upper or the bottom-wiper, that's where I will draw the line!

CHAPTER ELEVEN

Time to Quit?

Recently, an irate reader let me know he was sick of me moaning about my job as a flight attendant. His exact words were, "If you don't like it, the last I heard, the drink-tosser's job was voluntary."

I think he had the wrong opinion of my attitude toward the job, but he got me thinking about signs to look out for in the future. So, I drew up an informal poll and asked more than a hundred flight attendants when they would know it was time to take off their wings. Here are some of the best and most interesting answers:

You know it's time to quit being a flight attendant when:

- The co-pilot and the captain are both younger than you.

- You can remember when they cooked eggs to order in First Class.

- Passengers ask you questions at the airport and you aren't even in uniform.

- You see a passenger for the first time and know what he wants to drink even before he asks. (I am correct about 90 percent of the time. Some people just look like a ginger ale.)

- You wake up in a strange city, don't remember where you are, and don't really care.

- Your "secret knock" at home is the same as the code for the cockpit door.

- You have a huge collection of miniature alcohol bottles at home. (At last count, I had 512 miniatures from more than 50 countries.)

- You take alcohol off the airplane, and you aren't a drinker.

- You use the seat backs as support to walk down the aisles. Bless her heart, I flew with an 82-year-old flight attendant who needed the bar cart to prop her up in the aisle.

- A younger crew member asks you what it was like in the "good old days."

- Several hotel staffs know you by name.

- You're the last one to sit down to your family dinner, and the first one to clear the plates.

- You know the safety demonstration announcements by heart, and you prove it by reciting them in the shower.

- You have airplane disaster dreams, and you like them.

- You carry a non-uniform jacket with you just in case the day is full of cancellations and you will need to hide from angry passengers in the terminal.

- A younger crew member asks you if you still go out for drinks with the crew "at your age."

- You start to smell like a Boeing aircraft. *Eau de Boeing* they call it.

- You are serving dinner at home—it's either chicken or beef, and not very good—and you think about charging the family for it.

- When an angry passenger explains why he will never fly on your airline again, you agree with him and begin to wonder why anyone flies on your airline.

- You lie to perfect strangers about which airline you work for.

- You are on a tropical-island layover with beautiful weather and a fun crew, and you think the layover should be shorter so you can get home.

- On the way to work, you fantasize about phoning in a bomb threat just so your flight will be canceled.

- You see oversize luggage and you instinctively start to growl.

- Top management's bonuses increase, your paycheck and pension decrease, and you get curious about the going rate for hit men.

- You carry a flask everywhere you go.

- You start saying "Buh-bye" in your sleep.

Thanks to all my colleagues who answered the poll. Your responses were funny and insightful. As for me, I think it's time to quit being a flight attendant when you can no longer find the humor in the job. Luckily, that hasn't happened to me yet. I truly love this career, and I will stick it out—just to see what happens tomorrow.

PART FIVE

Being There

CHAPTER ONE

10 Tips for a Better Hotel Rest

H otels hold a very special place in every flight attendant's heart. They are the places where we rest our heads after a long day's work. Most crewmembers will stay in at least one hotel every time they go to work.

We have odd hotel hours. We might check in at 2 a.m. and check out at 10 p.m., so getting a good night's sleep may be a challenge. For example, at 8 a.m. the "attack" of the morning staff begins. The house-keeping army is on full offensive (and fully offensive). The whining and banging of vacuums, slamming of doors, and the yelling of in-structions to one another are enough to drive you crazy.

In Europe, I have been awakened many times by hotel staff checking for a depleted mini-bar. Can you imagine waking up to some strange man at the foot of your bed counting drinks? The "Do Not Disturb" sign may be on the door, but that minibar counter seems to have a waiver.

I value sleep immensely, so through the years I have gathered some tricks to the art of sleeping away from home. The following is a list of tips for a happier hotel rest:

1. **Room choice.** Don't get a room by the elevator or ice machine. You will feel the vibration all night long. It may not be apparent at first, but, believe me, when the lights are out, it will be. One more thing: if the hotel has a disco, make sure you get a room at least two floors away. I can't tell you how many nights in South America I tried to sleep to the beat.

2. **Do Not Disturb sign.** If your room does not have one, call the concierge or make one out of the hotel stationary paper. Without it, housekeeping will drive you bananas in the morning. I've lost count of the number of times a maid has caught me as I stumbled to the bathroom, naked.

3. **Earplugs.** Yes, my top in-flight tip is also one of my top hotel tips. It's very important that you get used wearing them. Put them by the bedside table. Bring a back-up pair, just in case.

4. **Party time.** If there is a party going on next door, do not, and I repeat, do not call security on the assumption they will solve the matter. Instead, I recommend packing your bags, returning to the front desk, and requesting another room. It's very easy for the front desk to say that they have no more rooms on the phone, but much more difficult to say it in person. If you feel inconvenienced by the revelers, you could always remember their room number and then give them a call early the next morning. They are bound to be in mid-sleep with a hangover waiting. The same goes for the loud couple next door going for the sexual marathon record. It's fun to listen to for the first 10 minutes but will make you cringe when it goes on for hours.

5. **Television timer.** If there is a timer function on the remote control, set it no matter how awake you feel. Waking up to a horror or war movie on high volume is a scary experience.

6. **Operator.** Call the operator and ask for a "do not disturb" on your phone line. Wrong-number calls will abound and are apt to ruin your slumber. You can request a "do not disturb" until a certain time or until you call and cancel. Alternately, you can merely unplug your phone.

7. **Trailblazing.** Clear a path from the bed to the toilet. This is so you don't have to turn a light on or stub a toe on the way to your nightly visit.

8. **Liquids.** Keep a glass or, better yet, a bottle of water within hand reach. Looking for some in the middle of the night might ruin any chance of getting back to sleep.

9. **Curtains.** Close the curtains all the way so the sun doesn't wake you in the morning.

10. **Alarming.** Check to be sure that the alarm clock has been turned off. There are people who get a kick out of setting it for the middle of the night as a practical joke for the next guest. Not my type of humor, but it's out there.

If you value sleep as much as I do, these strategies are well worth considering. Sweet dreams!

CHAPTER TWO

Phone Home

irline crews are probably the most frugal bunch of professionals out there—all the more so since the last round of pay cuts. We are gone an average of three to four days a week and many of us have families, so long-distance communication is a necessity. But when we call home from overseas, it costs us anywhere from 75 cents to $5 a minute. I remember a flight attendant who once called her fiance direct from South America, lost track of the time, and ended up owing more than $300 for the call. She cried uncontrollably when she saw her bill. Oh sure, you can get a calling card and dial a bunch of access codes from a cold phone booth for a little less, but it's still a hassle. Or you can bring your laptop and Instant Message each other, but "How r u?" doesn't really cut it, either.

When I became a new daddy last year, I realized it was time for me to embrace some more modern telecommunications technology. Recently, while I was in Kuwait for a week, I decided to give the Internet program Skype a try. I'd heard about it from other crewmembers, who touted it as a free computer-to-computer phone program capable of quality video. But I was skeptical. I'd seen earlier attempts at video phones and had been unimpressed. The video and audio quality was often poor, the setup was usually complicated, and I felt like a demented version of Max Headroom whenever I tried it.

Still, I was motivated to give video phones another try, so I bought a set of cameras for my PC and laptop, set them up and signed up at Skype.com. The video and audio quality from Kuwait was excellent. My trip was much more enjoyable because I was able to see and speak with my family every day. My little boy even kissed the screen when I said good night to him at his bedtime. I was blown away.

The kicker to all of this is that the service is free. No strings attached. (The free service is from computer to computer; if you want to call to a phone, get the SkypeOut package, which charges a small fee, like 2 cents a minute worldwide.) All you need is an Internet connection, a laptop and a small camera with a microphone. If you don't want to bring your laptop on your trip, you can go to any Internet cafe, plug a small phone into the USB port, and talk away. Some Internet cafes make these special phones available but, in my opinion, it's not as great as talking from the comfort of your hotel room and seeing your kid face to face.

Here are a couple of observations and tips for video conferencing from this new fan:

1. The slower the connection, the worse the quality. A dial-up connection doesn't work well and isn't really worth it.

2. Don't be afraid of the technical details. I find the instructions are pretty self-explanatory, and if I can do it, you can do it.

3. Turn off any background noises, such as the television or radio. They will play havoc with your audio transmission.

4. The lighting in front of you is more important than the lighting behind you.

5. Don't get frustrated. If at first you don't succeed, try, try again.

6. If you have a choice of a cable or WiFi, go with cable. It's generally faster.

7. Arrange your meeting time in advance, and have a backup time in case of unexpected events.

8. Remember, you are in front of a camera and the other person can see you. Once, when I was speaking to a female friend, I stood up to get something and then realized I had no pants on. Oops!

So, no more worrying about your family or shelling out a lot of money for pricey phone calls. Skype's got your number. And no, I'm not being paid by Skype. I'm just hooked, and I'll never travel without it again.

CHAPTER THREE

Best and Worst Travel Sayings Ever

When you fly into a new destination, you often hear some saying about it. It could be a motto, like "The Windy City" for Chicago, or a sly turn of phrase, like "City of Lost Wages" for Las Vegas. Here are some of my favorite travel sayings: good, bad, and ugly.

Let's start with some sayings that have grown old to me. If you haven't heard them before, enjoy. If you have, then groan along with me.

- **Denver.** "If you don't like the weather, wait a minute." Cute and true, but three hundred times? Enough already. Besides, I've heard it said about half a dozen other places.

- **San Francisco.** "The coldest winter I ever spent was a summer in San Francisco." Besides being confusing, it doesn't make a whole lot of sense to me. Mark Twain, the alleged commentator, must have been nipping at his brandy when he uttered that famous remark.

- **Phoenix, Arizona.** "But it's a dry heat." Phoenix certainly does lie in a hot region. So hot, in fact, that the average temperature in the summer is over 100 degrees. If I open my eyes and the air singes my eyeballs, I don't give a crap if it is a "dry heat"—it's still bloody hot! In Alaska, do they excuse their cold weather with, "But it's a dry cold"?

- **Australia.** "The toilet water flushes in the reverse direction because it is south of the equator." Whether it's true or not isn't the point. It's hard to find a toilet in Australia that flushes in a swirling motion to begin with. And then when I do, I always forget which way it swirls back in the States. So there I stand, feeling stupid, hunched over a toilet watching the direction of the whirlpool. "G'day, mate!"

- **Singapore.** "It's a fine city." There are fines for littering, spitting, and even chewing gum in public. I like Singapore, but I find the lack of diversity boring. To me, it is a fine but sterile city.

- **Greenland.** It's not. And Iceland isn't, either. Every time I fly over these two places, I figure the Vikings just mixed them up on their maps.

Now here are some state and city mottoes that puzzle me:

- **New Jersey:** "The Garden State." I have to admit I haven't seen many gardens in New Jersey. Maybe I just wasn't looking hard enough.

- **Florida:** "The Sunshine State." What a crock. It rains more there than anywhere in America, except Seattle. "The Sunshine State?" More like "The Soggy State."

- **Beaver, Oklahoma:** "Cow Chip Capital." Is this a good thing? Careful where you step?

- **Reno, Nevada:** "The Biggest Little City in the World." I get confused every time I think about it. And how did Reno qualify for the title, anyway?

- **San Francisco:** "Baghdad by the Bay." Who knew that one would come back to haunt them?

- **Oregon City, Oregon:** "The End is Just the Beginning." It sounds like someone has been smoking the plants over there.

- **Buffalo, New York:** "It's Good for You." What? Six feet of snow?

- **Austin, Minnesota:** "Spamtown, U.S.A." So that's where all those Viagra pushers live.

- **Fredericksburg, Virginia:** "Where History Never Gets Old." Actually, I like this one.

In my search for state mottoes, I stumbled upon some humorous ones. I mention them here in fun, with no intent to offend.

- **California:** "Se habla espanol."

- **Connecticut:** "The 'C' is Silent. No, the Other One."

- **Florida:** "The Gunshine State."

- **Idaho:** "Cogito Ergo Spud: I Think, Therefore I Yam."

- **Kentucky:** "Tobacco is a Vegetable."

- **Missouri:** "Missouri Loves Company."

- **Montana:** "More Cows Than People."

- **Ohio:** "Don't Judge Us by Cleveland."

- **South Carolina:** "Just South of North Carolina."

- **South Dakota:** "Closer Than North Dakota."

- **Vermont:** "Bet You Can't Name Two of Our Cities."

- **Washington:** "Come for the Protests, Stay for the Coffee!"

- **West Virginia:** "It's All Relative."

- **Wisconsin:** "Cutting the Cheese Since 1848."

There are many more, but I am sure that I have offended enough people by now. And just so you'll know I'm not a heartless cynic, here are my favorite travel sayings, the ones that I never get tired of:

- "Life is a journey, not a destination."
- "A traveler without observation is a bird without wings."
- "He who runs fastest doesn't always arrive first."
- "The most difficult step of any journey is the first."
- "The best journeys are not always in straight lines."
- "One time seen is better than one hundred times heard about." (Czech saying)
- "A journey is like marriage. The certain way to be wrong is to think you control it." (John Steinbeck)
- "I'm not lost, I've just temporarily lost sight of my destination."
- "Not all who wander are lost." (J. R. R. Tolkien)
- And my personal favorite: "When traveling, he who laughs, lasts."

CHAPTER FOUR

Tourist Written All Over You

Have you ever wondered how local people always seem to know you're a tourist when you are traveling abroad? To tell you the truth, it's not rocket science. I'm not a local, I'm an American, and I can spot a fellow tourist from a mile away. Apart from the obvious differences, like our Yankee English and our baseball caps, there are 10 dead giveaways that the individual in front of you hails from the U-S-of-A.

And here they are.

1. **Clothes make the tourist.** White tennis shoes almost always announce an American tourist, just as black socks with shorts identify a British tourist. Sweatshirts with university names, baseball

caps, cowboy hats, and Hawaiian shirts are other signs that you are American.

2. **Map quest.** You know you've spotted a American tourist when you seem him standing in the middle of a busy thoroughfare, consulting a city map with a puzzled look fixed to his face. No, sir, you're not in Kansas anymore.

3. **Wallet check.** Americans like to keep their wallets in their back pockets. This is not a safe practice, and they seem to be aware of it, because most Americans abroad have the habit of tapping their wallet every so often, just to make sure it's still there. Sadly, the habit is useless. I had my wallet stolen from me once and I never felt a thing. If your wallet gets lifted, the perpetrators will be long gone before you know it, and no amount of tapping is going to change that.

4. **Center of the universe.** For some reason, American tourists are extra-loud both in action and in words. True, they are on vacation and looking for fun, but they don't have to yell at each other while doing it: "IS THE MOW-NA LISA SUPPOSED TO BE ON THIS FLO-WOR?"

5. **Creatures of habit.** Whether it is McDonald's in Greece, The Olive Garden in Rome, or Starbucks in Lebanon, Americans tend to flock to familiar names when hunger or thirst sets in abroad. Once in a while, I do it too. Comfort food, I guess.

6. **Feeling flush.** When American tourists enter foreign toilet facilities for the first time, they are generally overcome with confusion and wonderment. Whether they've encountered an infrared automatic flush, a pull-chain handle, a hole in the ground, or a bidet, you can bet their first remark upon exiting will be, "You won't believe what they've got in there!"

7. **Friend to all.** Aside from the occasional American grouch, Americans are generally a friendly folk. When they are abroad, they are the first to say "Howdy," to ask you to take their picture, to look on a stranger's plate in a restaurant and ask what the food is and whether it tastes good. Unfortunately, many foreign cultures consider this behavior to be overly familiar.

8. **Say cheese.** Taking pictures is a fact of tourism, but how many pictures do you really need of the homeless man in the corner or the shopkeeper setting up his fruit stand? Tourists will take countless pictures of trivial things, but I guess beauty is in the eye of the clicker.

9. **Super sleuth.** Before committing to a restaurant, many American tourists will pass by it several times, each time scoping out the menu, sizing up the clientele, and taking notes on what the customers are eating. I once counted 13 pass-bys from a tourist family of five.

10. **Regular guy.** For some reason, bowel movements are often the subject of American tourists' conversation and are considered a perfectly suitable topic for breakfast-table discussion. Not only that, other Americans who overhear these discussions will often join into the conversation—with enthusiasm!

Being a tourist is nothing to be ashamed of; in fact, I give credit to every American who ventures beyond the snug comfort of his American armchair. But some Americans' behavior abroad is nothing to be proud of, either, and we might be more careful how we present ourselves, especially these days, when the world's opinion of the United States is so mixed. So maybe check your clothes in the mirror, step out of the traffic, turn down the volume, put down that Big Mac, and make an effort to appreciate local customs and sensibilities.

But to tell you the truth, even after all such attempts to buff up your image, the locals will still know you're a tourist. The vendors will still make a special trip outside their shop to try to sell you something, and strangers will still ask you where you are from. When that happens, I have an answer. Now, I am very proud of my country, but I'm not too interested in getting into another debate over the Iraq conflict or the ethics of George Bush, so in potentially hostile situations, I usually reply, "Canada." With that, the conversation or the haggling ends.

CHAPTER FIVE

10 Money-Savers for Travelers

A irline crews are experts at avoiding incidental charges. Some say we're cheap; others say we are just frugal. Now that our paychecks and pensions have been slashed, economy is a necessity. Besides, why throw money away if you don't have to? Here are 10 common nickel-and-dime travel charges, along with a few suggestions on how to avoid them.

1. **Car rental insurance.** You're out of town and the agent asks you, "Would you like collision coverage for your rental?" Then, when you say no, the agent tries to scare you into second-guessing your choice. (Sometimes the cost of the insurance is as much as the car rental!) What you should know is that your own auto insurance probably covers that rental car, so before you head out on your next trip, give your insurance agent a call. Also, many credit cards extend insurance coverage if you use that credit card for the car rental. Many people think this coverage is bogus, but it's not. Last

winter a friend of mine returned from a day of skiing to find his rental car was the victim of a hit-and-run. His credit card company covered the entire expense.

2. **Hotel parking.** Think you got a sweet deal on that hotel? Think again. Many hotels charge as much as $20 a night for parking, which I think is a rip-off considering hotel prices are so high these days. So, before you confirm that reservation, ask if there is free parking for guests.

3. **Next-day tickets.** You learn at the last minute that you need to travel tomorrow for some important event. Airlines typically charge astronomical fares for next-day flights. They do this because they know you are desperate and that you will pay almost anything. Don't pay those fares without first doing an Internet search, which can sometimes turn up some surprising last-minute specials. A friend of mine once needed a ticket for a flight to Los Angeles in less than four hours time. He found one on <u>Lowestfare. com</u> for $200 when the airline was trying to charge him $900.

4. **Hidden fees.** Have you ever checked your ticket invoice and counted up the hidden fees? There can be fees for airport construction, security, and airport access, not to mention excise and customs charges, gate taxes, country taxes, value-added taxes, and even 9/11 charges. Personally, I am surprised not to find an Overpaid Airline Executive fee. There is no way to avoid paying these taxes and fees, but I understand they are all tax-deductible. If you travel enough, they can add up to quite a bit.

5. **The useless upgrade (part 1).** Some airlines are now charging extra for some aisle seats and window seats or for the roomier seats in economy. An agent will ask you at check-in if you are interested in paying a nominal fee for one of these seats. Before you take out your wallet, ask if the flight is oversold, because if it's not, you may be paying for something you can have for free. Mind you, if your flight is full and more than two hours long, the extra cost might just be worth it.

6. **The useless upgrade (part 2).** How many times have you gone to a car rental agency and been offered a great deal on a fancier car?

What the agent isn't telling you is that they've run out of compact cars (like the one you booked), and they're hoping to turn their little oops into a moneymaking opportunity. If you decline the "upgrade," they have to give you the nicer car anyway, and you drive away happy. Also steer clear of the "pay-now-and-bring-the-car-back-empty" scam. Studies have shown that 9 times out of 10 you lose money with that deal. I purposely drove out of my way once just to empty the tank and ended up feeling like a fool.

7. **H_2O to go.** The price of bottled water can be astronomically high at hotels, but when you get to your room you just don't want to risk the tap water. So, just fill up your empty bottle at the hotel gym. While you're at it, have a workout. Double bonus!

8. **Mini-bar, maxi price**. Have you ever been tempted by the offerings of the in-room mini-bar at the hotel, but scared straight when you saw the mini-bar prices? Go ahead and indulge, but be sure you replace the item from the local store at a tenth of the price. Be sure the mini-bar does not have the automatic sensors that add any moved item to your room bill. There should be adequate signs on the outside.

9. **Drink specials.** I don't care if it makes you look cheap, always ask about drink specials before ordering. I can't count the number of times I've paid twice as much for a smaller drink when the larger one was on special. Also, if you drink only one brand of liquor—say, Jack Daniels—ask the server what the house bourbon is before you place your order. If it's Jack Daniels, you can order a bourbon and coke and pay less than if you had specified Jack Daniels in the first place.

10. **Sky-high Wi-Fi.** Most airports and hotels charge for wireless Internet access, and it can cost up to $20 just to check your e-mail. But many hotel lobbies offer Wi-Fi for free.

It's good to treat yourself once in a while, but when you travel as much as I do, small items add up. By following some of these tips, you could save enough to splurge on that $10 overpriced airport coffee drink. But that's another chapter altogether.

CHAPTER SIX

Spring Break Mistake

A couple of years ago, my wife and I decided to take a week off and fly to some romantic destination with the idea of starting a family. Winter had been especially stressful that year, as my wife, who is a pilot, had recently been promoted to captain, and I was trying to juggle three jobs at once.

While recovering from a morning spent shoveling snow from my driveway, I thought of a hot destination: Cancun. Sure, it's somewhat touristy, but neither of us had ever been there, and I was thinking of that Corona commercial—you know, the one with the palm trees and the beach. All I wanted was some peace, relaxation, and a little good fortune.

My wife met me at the airport after her working flight. I had brought her packed bag, and our travel plans were right on schedule. One of the flight attendants recognized me as a colleague and remarked, "You're going to Cancun now? Good luck."

What did she mean, "Good luck"? We were already on our way, and we had a nice, inexpensive hotel already booked. Luck? Who needed luck?

I looked around and did notice that we were one of the oldest couples on-board, but I shrugged it off. After all, Cancun is pretty much Beach Central. Then some surfer teenager straight out of a Bill & Ted movie sat down next to me and said, "Dude, are you one of the chaperones?"

I laughed it off, but it got me thinking.

I looked a little harder at the crowd. We were surrounded by teenagers dressed in their beach attire, acting like they were off to some sort of convention. My wife and I slowly put 2 and 2 together. Then, simultaneously, we looked at each other in horror and exclaimed, "Spring break!"

How could we have been so stupid? What were we thinking? We had gotten a good deal at an all-inclusive hotel with room, food, and —oh, no!—booze. If we hadn't already been in the air, we would have deplaned on the spot.

In the past, I have enjoyed many spring breaks. I have experienced the wild nights and suffered many hung-over mornings, but I was older now. I was past the wet T-shirt phase of my life. Maybe it would be different this time—less rowdy, more civilized—but something about being hit several times with pretzels during the flight made me doubt it.

We were the oldest people in the hotel check-in line by about 20 years. Eight boys shared the room to our right and six girls were on our left. Room parties and live bands went on until the wee hours of the morning; the local bus became the drunk shuttle; and everywhere I went I was called "Pops." The sidewalks in the morning were cluttered with passed-out revelers from the night before, not to mention the vomit and litter.

On the second night, we considered surrendering and going back home. But we would lose all of the hotel payment, and besides, it was wonderfully hot in Cancun and bitterly cold at home. It was give up or give in. The cheapskate side of us took over and we decided to make the best of a difficult situation.

So my wife and I relaxed a bit, enjoyed the festivities, and bathed in the sun. We posed as chaperones, helped out some neighbors who had too much to drink, and danced to the live bands. I even tried some Jell-O shots.

Here are a few things I learned from that trip about traveling during spring break season:

1. **Check the calendar.** Think twice about visiting tropical destinations anytime from mid-March to May—especially if you're looking for peace or romance.

2. **Get lost.** Rent a car or head for remote locations away from the partygoers. My wife and I took a boat to a small island off Cancun and snorkeled for two days. Heavenly bliss.

3. **Change your room.** Ask the concierge for a room away from it all. The desk felt sorry for us and changed our room halfway through our stay; otherwise, I think we'd have gone crazy.

4. **Spend some cash.** Think about the company you'll keep if price is the sole consideration when you book your hotel. We suffered for our thrift. Had we paid a little more, we might have avoided the spring break crowd and spent time with some actual adults.

5. **Plug them up.** Take your earplugs. I wore mine constantly in Cancun and still managed to hear much of the conversation and all of the music.

6. **Act your age.** Drinking games are not what they used to be. If you're not accustomed to shooters and beer pong, I suggest you give them a pass (this is a tip I wish I had followed myself).

7. **Get excluded.** Stay away from all-inclusive accommodations during this time—they are magnets for kids. Besides, the all-inclusive setup keeps you from exploring the many different restaurants and cultures that await you in town.

8. **If you can't beat 'em, join 'em.** Go with the flow and try to make the best of spring break. There is always a way to have fun, and it only comes around once a year.

Had we gone home, my wife and I would have missed out on an unusual adventure. No, we are not planning to go back to Cancun during spring break, but we did enjoy ourselves. Plus, while we aren't 100 percent positive, we believe our little boy got his start on spring break in Cancun. I even suggested Corona as his middle name, but that idea was vetoed almost immediately.

CHAPTER SEVEN

That Free Drink Could Be Your Last

love my job as a flight attendant. I travel all over the world, enjoy several days a month in foreign locations, and try to take advantage of the perks of my career. I consider myself travel-savvy so I write travel tips, funny and serious. When I get caught doing something foolish, I am usually quick to admit it, and I pass along any lessons learned to my readers.

But one time I didn't. Something happened to me a couple of years back that scared me half to death, and it is only recently that I have come to full terms with the ordeal.

I was in Brazil at a nightclub where a jazz band I liked was scheduled to play. The crewmember I'd come with got tired and decided to go back to the hotel. That's when it happened.

One moment I was drinking and talking with a couple of exchange students, and the next moment I was physically impaired. It was as if everything had switched to slow motion, as if my movements and reactions were grinding to a halt. I have been drunk before, but this was different. I had been drugged. I was in trouble, and I had to get back to the hotel as soon as possible. I staggered outside and tried to flag down a cab, but I could hardly walk straight.

A stranger approached and guided me into an alleyway. I thought he was trying to help me, but no. There were others waiting in the alley. They pushed me to the ground, kicked me a few times, and proceeded to check my pockets. All the while, I was helpless. I was unable to defend myself, run, or even scream for help. The attackers took my wallet, which contained a little money, one bank card, and my driver's license.

"What's your bank number?" one of the men shouted at me repeatedly. I couldn't tell him. I wasn't sure of my own name much less my bank code. They kicked me some more. The last thing I remember is my attackers running away. Unable to move, I first wept, then passed out.

I awoke very early the next morning to the sound of street cleaners. I looked around and saw that my shoes, wallet, and jacket were gone. My side hurt. As crazy as this sounds, I checked to see if my kidneys were still there. I had heard stories about organ thieves in South America, and I had to make sure I was still intact. I tried to flag down a cab, but who was going to pick up a fare with no shoes? Finally a taxi stopped, and I waited until I got to the hotel to tell the cabbie I had no wallet.

I got to my room and slept for the next 20 hours. I had nightmares. When I woke up, I took a two-hour shower.

It was then I decided I wouldn't tell anyone about my ordeal. I would pretend it had never happened. I was embarrassed, ashamed, and haunted by the whole matter, and I didn't want to share those feelings with anyone. It worked OK at first, but after waking up night after night in a cold sweat, I had to tell my wife. By telling her, the demons slowly retreated and my life gradually returned to normal.

Until a couple of months ago.

That's when my airline made an announcement about a flight attendant who had been drugged on a layover in Germany with Rohypnol, or "roofies," a powerful sedative that is also called the "date-rape drug." The woman had been robbed and sexually assaulted, and she was in the hospital.

My own ordeal came back to haunt me, and I felt guilty for remaining silent. Maybe I could have prevented this woman's attack by openly telling about mine.

Well, I am speaking up now, to tell everyone that this type of crime is out there and to offer the following advice:

1. **Say no to freebies.** If you don't know where the drink came from, decline it.

2. **Buddy up.** Never leave alone—or be left alone—in a foreign place at night. I knew better. I should have gone back to the hotel with my crew mate.

3. **Call the police.** They probably won't catch the perpetrators, but your episode will be logged. Multiple reports may get the justice wheels rolling, especially if the incidents start to hurt tourism.

4. **Speak up.** Don't hide your ordeal; tell others. Your misfortune could save them.

5. **Go for counseling.** If you can't find mental and emotional relief, seek help. But know that the pain and nightmares might never quite go away.

I recently went out on an experiment. On an international layover, I sent 10 strangers anonymous drinks, and nine of the people drank them. The only one who declined gave it to her friend—and she drank it. Take it from me, this trusting acceptance of free gifts from strangers is more dangerous than you could ever imagine.

This is my therapy, and I feel better by passing the word. It might be a bit late, but if I can prevent just one similar experience, this chapter will have served its purpose. Take care of yourself out there. Enjoy life. But use some common sense.

Safety First, Fondue Later

My luck in Paris has not been what one would call great. I have had a bad case of poison ivy, suffered severely from food poisoning, and was a passenger in the worst car accident of my life—all in Paris. You'd think with my track record, I would try to avoid that region of the world. But I can't. I'm a flight attendant.

And anyway, I love Paris, and France is one of my favorite destinations. My wife speaks French; we fell in love in Bordeaux; and some of our fondest holiday memories are from France. But let me tell you a cautionary tale.

I was on a layover in Paris in the springtime, and I wanted to share this beautiful city with some friends on the crew. After a full day of sightseeing, I treated two female co-workers to a secret fondue place in the Montmartre district (Refuge du Fondue). We had stuffed our faces with a delicious cheese feast and had indulged in far too much red wine from large baby bottles. Although it was getting late, one of my friends suggested we head to Sacre-Coeur, which was a steep uphill climb a half-mile away. We needed the exercise after that meal, anyway.

Almost to the top and out of breath, we had one last stretch of steps to go. All of a sudden, one of my friends shrieked as two men walking down the steps grabbed her purse. One slit the purse strap with a knife and the other tugged it free. It all happened in an instant, and before I knew it, I was in a foot chase with two thugs. They saw me chasing, so they split up at the bottom of the steps.

I continued to chase the one with the purse tucked under his arm. It had started to rain lightly, and the cobblestones had become quite slippery. I tripped a couple of times but, luckily, so did our assailant. The chase continued through the back streets of Paris and across a few busy streets. I was actually catching up to the guy when we ran into a back alley. It was a dead end, and suddenly he was cornered.

Now what?, I thought to myself as the man slowly turned around and took out his knife. That was enough for me. I turned to run away but was greeted by three of his friends. "Take out your wallet and throw it to me," one of them shouted in broken French. "Can't we talk about this, guys? I replied. One of them smirked, "He wants to talk?"

They continued to walk toward me and I began to yell for help. I felt a blow to the back of my head as one of them hit me from behind.

I woke up in a hospital bed with the mother of all headaches. I was sore from head to toe, and my face had what can only be described as a footmark indentation, but luckily there was no knife cut. Best of all, I was alive.

The following are some safety tips I learned from this experience (and from other somewhat less adventurous layovers). They should be helpful to everyone traveling abroad.

1. **When sightseeing, always bring a small purse or wallet, and put only the bare essentials in it**: one credit card, one piece of photo identification, and enough cash for the intended outing. Leave everything else in your hotel room or in the hotel safe. If

you insist on carrying your passport with you, purchase a pouch that straps to your body. The woman's purse that was stolen was a stripped down purse that contained nothing too valuable; unfortunately, my wallet had everything in it.

2. **Always keep your wallet in your front pocket** and your purse around your opposite shoulder with the opening facing inward, toward your body.

3. **If you encounter someone trying to take your purse or wallet, yell loudly.** The attention may scare the purse-snatcher away.

4. **Don't resist.** If you struggle too hard, you could get seriously hurt. Remember, the man has cut your purse strap with something that can cut you just as easily.

5. **Don't be a hero.** I learned this the hard way. I was the only male, and I felt it was my duty to catch the assailants. That was misplaced chivalry. Besides being beaten up and almost hit by two cars, I lost my wallet. Worse, I could have been killed.

6. **If someone threatens you and demands your wallet or purse, just hand it over.** Remember, it's only a leather contraption that holds your personal items, and most of those can be replaced. Your life can't be.

7. **Guard your drinks.** A recent criminal ploy is to spike drinks with Rohypnol, better known as "roofies." Yes, this is the date-rape drug, but it can also be slipped into the drinks of unsuspecting tourists. I know many crewmembers who have become victims of this dangerous drug.

8. **Never write your room number on the sleeve of your hotel key card.** If you've had too much wine and have forgotten the details of your room assignment, just go to the front desk and ask. Believe me, they are used to it. I like this option much better then finding some stranger in my room.

9. **Don't assume that the person lying on the side of a back street is a homeless person.** Apparently, the French lady who found me mistook me for a vagrant. (This is understandable since I was unconscious, smelled like booze, and my clothes were all messed

up.) Luckily, she called the police anyway. Do the same for the next poor sod, or at least notify a nearby shopkeeper.

10. **Trust your first instincts.** I wasn't too happy with the late hour of our last sightseeing tour, but decided I was being overprotective of my friends. I went along with the consensus, never voicing my concern. Big mistake.

This advice should be followed in every major city. Crime is a fact of life, and your awareness and safety precautions are your first defense.

My wife and I are planning a trip to France soon, beginning with a weekend in Paris. I am a bit leery, but I'm looking forward to walking those beautiful streets again. This time, I will be better prepared.

First stop, fondue!

8 Steamy Sauna Tips

O ne December, many years ago, I had a whole month of flight assignments to Berlin. On an especially cold winter day, I decided to stay in the hotel for the duration of the layover. Christmas was approaching and I wanted to rest up for the holiday season. I had heard the hotel had the best sauna in Europe, so I decided to check it out. A sauna might be therapeutic, I thought.

Whenever I'm abroad, I try to follow local customs. In the locker room, I noticed that the men walking in from the sauna were naked. I figured there were separate saunas for men and women, so I followed suit—or I should say, suit-less. The sauna consisted of seven different sections, each with specific instructions for use. For maximum results, the user should stay in each section for 10 minutes and then move on to the next station. I was given a timer that would go off every 10 minutes.

I walked into the first station, which was a eucalyptus steam room, designed to open the pores. I removed my towel and reveled in the heat. There is something decadent about sitting in a sauna when you know it's snowing outside. A few minutes later, the door opened and five female Alitalia Airlines flight attendants walked in. I knew they worked for Alitalia because I had seen them in the hotel lobby when I checked in. My first thought was that I was in the women's sauna and they were about to scream. Stretched out, butt naked and fearing their reaction, I quickly closed my legs.

To my surprise, they hardly took notice of me and removed their towels. So there I was, 22 years old, naked in a sauna with five equally naked Italian women, praying with all my might that an embarrassing body reaction was not about to take place. I had lived in Germany for a few years before taking the airline job, and had learned, somewhat, to deprogram the taboo about public nudity that I grew up with in America. Still, I was a young man at my sexual peak and this was going to be hard (no pun intended).

Somehow, I started to relax, and my fears began to fade. I felt wonderful, not in a sexual way, but in a peaceful way. I was in a room of naked people, without issues or uneasy feelings. It felt totally natural. Then my timer went off and everyone turned and stared at me. I got up and moved on to the second room.

This room was an extremely hot sauna with the smell of lavender. I relaxed, and sure enough three minutes later the five young ladies joined me. Each one was beautiful in her own way, with a different shape and distinctive characteristics.

The pattern of advancing through the rooms continued for the next three stations. We didn't bother putting our towels back on between rooms, and I even managed to carry on a short conversation with a couple of the women. There were no incidents of blood rushing to the wrong part of my body as previously feared. Maybe I was growing up. I got to the sixth section, which consisted of stairs leading up to a small plunge pool. According to the instructions, I was to immerse myself in the cold water and jump up and down, splashing water over my body. I was proud of my newfound maturity, but cold water and a naked man do not mix. I skipped the sixth station and headed for number seven.

This section was a sauna with a glass front looking out on the plunge pool. One by one, my lovely Italian sauna mates took their turns jumping in and splashing. There I was, facing out with nowhere else to look. It was as if I had front-row tickets at a show. I guess I could have closed my eyes but I didn't think of that. Instead, I wondered: Who designed this layout? By the time the fourth plunge-pool contestant jumped in, my youthful vigor won the day, and no number of depressing thoughts would change the matter. I wrapped the towel around me and made my escape.

It was a great sauna, but was it "therapeutic"? Not exactly: I had difficulty sleeping and concentrating for the rest of the layover.

Here are some tips for enjoying saunas abroad:

1. **Make inquiries.** Your hotel might have a wonderful sauna and gym, but if you don't ask, you'll never know.

2. **Give it a try.** If you get an opportunity to take a similar sauna, go for it. It might be the highlight of your trip.

3. **Ask about the dress code.** Don't assume anything. It may be clothing optional, clothing (or towel) mandatory, or even clothing not allowed.

4. **Grin and bare it**. If it is clothing optional, do as the Romans do. Everyone is self-conscious about one thing or another, but you should never be embarrassed of your body. Celebrate the differences and shed your hang-ups with your clothes. You will probably find the experience soul-gratifying and quite liberating.

5. **Think before you sit.** If you sit down with a bare behind, put a towel down, or you might burn more than you bargained for. And if you do go into the eucalyptus room, bring tissues, because your nose is sure to run.

6. **Take on water.** Don't buy a bottle of water to drink when you work out. Instead, bring an empty bottle and fill it up from the hotel's purified supply.

7. **Get a massage.** You are away from home, and stressed from business or a hectic itinerary, so why not get a massage? Your hotel

may offer deals for its guests. If not, spend a little extra on yourself. You're worth it.

8. **Delay happy hour.** Instead of meeting up with your colleagues or travel companions right away, go to the hotel gym for 30 minutes—whether there's a sauna or not. A short workout will cut down on jet lag and mitigate any hangover you might get.

A sauna can be just the thing after a long flight. Just sit back, relax, and let the heat and relaxation work out any kinks that the cramped airplane seats may have caused. But, mature or not, I still recommend that all naked men headed for the sauna stay away from the cold-water pool.

CHAPTER TEN

Surviving Oktoberfest

I got to my first Oktoberfest on a lucky break, landing a five-day gig as a trumpet player in one of the beer tents in Munich. I've gone nine times since, and I considered myself something of a beer-drinking genius, until two years ago, when I met an old-timer named Clay.

I'm no longer a trumpet player by profession; I'm a flight attendant—a useful occupation should you want to travel once a year to Germany to savor some excellent brew. Unfortunately, Munich flights generally go only to very senior crewmembers, and with only 16 years on the job at that time, I wasn't even close.

But begging paid off, and I was ecstatic: I had a 30-hour layover in Munich, leaving me plenty of time to indulge. The only drawback was the rather elderly company; I figured my co-workers probably came with bad backs and canes. But I was determined to enjoy the festival—no matter what.

On the bus to the hotel, Edith, the purser, invited me to the beer fest with the rest of the crew. I really wanted to go solo so I could search out a younger crowd, but I was polite.

"Sure," I said, knowing I could always sneak out the back door. "You all fancy a beer, do you?"

Everyone chuckled as Clay, the oldest male flight attendant I have ever seen, replied, "Son, I will drink you under the table."

Clearly, Clay didn't know who he was dealing with, but his remark was a sign that he might be good company.

When we arrived at the festival grounds, Edith pointed out some attractions of interest and outlined the plan of action. She ended with a caution: "Be careful. Oktoberfest beer is strong." I figured the geezers would go for a stein, then switch to Coke for the rest of the night.

Not at all. They started ordering beers left and right. We went from tent to tent, drinking, eating snacks and enjoying ourselves. I hate to admit it, but I was having some trouble keeping up with Clay. The night progressed joyously. I was going to teach the group the drinking songs, but they already knew them. They also knew the associated dances and performed them on top of the tables.

Do you wonder what ever happened to all those John Denver songs? Well, they were alive and well in Munich that year, when thousands of patrons from all over the world (including, oddly enough, me) screamed out several renditions of "Country Roads" and "Rocky Mountain High." We also danced the Chicken Dance to the many toasting songs of "Ein Prosit!"

Why, this was the hippest older crew I had ever flown with! We sang with heart, drank arm-in-arm, and swayed back and forth with friendly folks from other tables. I was having the greatest time when, all of a sudden, I found I was unspeakably drunk.

I awoke the next morning in the hotel room with my head pounding and my tongue rasping my mouth like a dry sponge. I had no recollection of how I had gotten back to the hotel. The last thing I remembered was doing the Chicken Dance with Clay.

My hangover settled in on the bus to the airport. Around me, the rest of the crew was perky. I started to turn green, and it wasn't from envy. Edith let me know I'd been fine until the end of the evening, when I started talking nonsense. She and Alberta later found me passed out in front of my hotel room door. I had the key in my hand but was apparently unable to make it work, so they had helped me up and in.

"Wait a minute," I objected. "I woke up in my underwear."

"Yes, dear, we helped you with that as well," Alberta said. "Oh, please, we have grandchildren older than you. But I must say that you are quite fit."

Then she winked at me.

Lest you find yourself in this situation, I offer the following tips for surviving Oktoberfest. The Munich Oktoberfest takes place the last two weeks of September and the first week of October; elsewhere, Oktoberfests can run through the end of the month.

1. **First and foremost, beware!** The October brew is, indeed, stronger than regular German beer (which is already strong by American standards), and it usually comes in oversized mugs that hold four to six servings. Exercise extreme caution when ordering more than two of these.

2. **Pick a meeting place.** Choose a meeting place in case you get separated from your companions. Beer festivals are very crowded places. Add a few high-powered drinks and a lot of excitement, and the chances of getting lost rise exponentially.

3. **Stoke your stomach.** Eat like there's no tomorrow, otherwise you will wish there were. Give the stomach something to soak up the beer. Sausages (bratwurst) are good for starters.

4. **Remember your table.** The tables in a beer fest tent all look pretty much alike, even when you're sober. So get your bearings first thing, and remember some landmark that will point you in the right direction when you return from the bathroom.

5. **Pace yourself.** Don't set out to get drunk. There's no need. You will wind up there no matter what.

6. **Go native.** If a German gentleman grabs your elbow and starts to sing and sway to the music, sway too.

7. **Who are you?** Leave your passport at the hotel but carry identification with you, just in case you forget who you are or the police catch you urinating on the sidewalk.

8. **Know your hotel.** Bring your hotel information with you in case you get separated from your party. Why? Because when the taxi driver asks you, "Which Sheraton?," you will have no idea.

9. **Stash some water.** Put a big bottle of water on your nightstand before you go to sleep. It will be worth millions when you wake in the wee hours.

10. **Plan for some recovery time.** Wait a day before getting on an airplane. There is nothing worse than flying with a hangover.

When the flight ended, I thanked everyone for a memorable Oktoberfest. I bowed to Clay, declared myself unworthy of his company, and high-tailed it home for a long, long slumber. I had a great time, but I realize now that I did myself a disservice by prejudging my crewmates. I wouldn't have had half the fun if I'd ventured out alone, and who knows what shape I would have turned up in.

My advice: Don't judge a book by its cover, no matter how old and worn the cover might be. It's the wisdom and experience inside that counts.

CHAPTER ELEVEN

On the Road to Beijing

I began flying a trans-Pacific route to China in 2007 and had my first three-day layover in Beijing in April. The capital of the most populous nation on earth, Beijing is a bustling city with some amazing history and culture—and some serious problems. It will be interesting to see how it pulls itself together for next year's Summer Olympic Games.

Let's start with some of the pros.

- The U.S. dollar is strong, which certainly is not the case in most foreign countries. And I mean really strong. For example, you can dine out with drinks for approximately $3-5 a person.

- There are many amazing tourist attractions to visit, such as the Forbidden City, the Great Wall, and more museums and cultural exhibits than you can see in a lifetime.

- Shopping. Have you ever noticed that most merchandise items have a "Made in China" notice affixed to them somewhere? Well, here you are in the land of cheap manufactured goods, and there are deals aplenty.

- The city is in the middle of an upgrade. Along every busy road you'll see rows and rows of boxed flowers. Thousands of young trees are being planted to improve air quality and to minimize the effects of sandstorms. Hundreds of buildings are under construction. I can't imagine they will be completed in time for next summer's festivities, but maybe the Chinese will prove me wrong.

- The cuisine—the price is right and so is the taste. "Peking Duck" is a must, but I was leery of the "Scorpion and Cricket Shish Kabob."

Now for some of the cons.

- Traffic constantly blocks the streets. Many new streets are being built for the upcoming summer games but for the time being, the construction only adds to the congestion.

- The smog is shocking. It clouds the air and hovers over the horizon, so that every day of touring was followed by sore eyes, itchy throat, congested sinuses, and the well-known "China cough." Is this a healthy environment for the biggest sporting event in the world? There are rumors that factories will shut down months before the Olympics, but you wonder how people cope on an everyday basis.

- You also have to wonder about human rights. I won't comment on a subject I don't know a lot about, but I did find it interesting that my 21-year-old language guide, who lived 10 miles outside of Beijing at the time of the Tiananmen Square massacre in

1989, had not heard about that event. He told us that unfavorable news did not spread quickly in China.

If you are planning a trip for the Olympics or just for a vacation, here are some tips that can help you enjoy your stay more.

1. **Get a massage.** There is nothing quite like a full-body massage after a 14-hour flight—or even just an extensive foot massage. And where else can you get a two-hour rubdown for just $13? Ask at your hotel for a reputable practitioner, or you might just get a surprise at the end!

2. **Be a tourist.** Visit the Great Wall (go early and avoid weekends if possible) and the Forbidden City (get a student guide but haggle the price down), and go to the Night Market and see Beijing lit up at night. These are excursions that you will remember for a lifetime.

3. **Get relief.** Bring your sinus, congestion, and cold medications to battle the sometimes nasty environment, especially if you are sensitive to pollution.

4. **H-2-Uh-Oh.** Stick to bottled water even in your hotel; most accommodations do not have potable water in the rooms. This goes for brushing your teeth, too. You should even exercise caution when showering—remember to keep your mouth closed!

5. **Shop till you drop.** Take a relatively empty suitcase and buy most of your clothes after you get to China. The big markets I know of are the Pearl, Silk, Toy and Night Markets, but wherever you shop, you will have fun and your dollar will go far.

6. **Going abroad.** Get mentally prepared for the infamous squatting toilets. It's not so bad once you get the hang of it. (Easy for me to say—I am a guy.)

7. **Taxi.** Make sure the cab you get into has a meter; otherwise the driver will take you for a ride in more ways than one.

8. **Venture out.** Try to minimize eating and drinking at hotel restaurants and bars. These are usually costly, they lack local flavor,

and the patrons are mostly other tourists. Get out, explore, and mingle with the masses.

One curious note: On the flight over to China there were not many babies, but the return flight had quite a few. I quickly learned that many American couples make the trek to China in search of adoptions. In my observation, they fly out with joy and hope in their hearts, and fly back with reality screaming in their ears. But I am sure in the new parents' case, they don't mind one bit.

The Olympic Games tend to change a city and sometimes not for the better. It will be interesting to see Beijing after its cosmetic upgrades have been completed. So far, I am optimistic, and I hope to see you at the Olympics!

CHAPTER TWELVE

Tales From the China Shop

N othing can quite prepare you for a daylong shopping spree in China. It starts out small with a knockoff shirt or two, then escalates to things you don't really need or want but the prices are just too good to pass up. Before you know it, you've bought a duffel bag just to lug around all the stuff you've proudly purchased.

Why do people—even grown men—do this? Because it's like Christmas, but at 90 percent off. And that's before you start the haggling. You can dance through the aisles buying high-end watches, shoes, bags, and jewelry for the wife. You can buy remote-control toys, electronic gadgets, tailor-made suits, and pearls by the truckload. You know half of it's fake and probably won't last very long, but who cares? You are like the proverbial kid in a candy store and you suddenly have a huge sweet tooth. You have been bitten by the shopping bug.

I know this because I recently went to Beijing, and I got caught up in a shopping spree. In fact, I came home with two duffel bags full of goodies. I also came home with some tips to pass on to travelers who are going shopping in China. And here they are.

1. **Try it on.** Don't believe the label. In China, sizes are often taped inside the garment. Twice when a shop didn't have the size I wanted, the shopkeeper disappeared and returned with the shirt in the correct size. I mean, the exact same shirt but with a different size label pasted on the inside.

2. **Caveat emptor.** Knockoffs can be great; they can look and feel like the real thing. But, remember, they are not the real thing, and they may not last or perform like the real thing. So while you're congratulating yourself for saving hundreds of dollars, don't expect too much.

3. **Keep moving.** For some reason, "Just looking" doesn't translate into Chinese. In fact, the vendors will hound you to buy all kinds of stuff you don't want. So if you're not interested in anything a shop has to offer, don't bother entering. Besides, there are so many shops and so little time.

4. **Think big.** When buying clothing, it is smart to buy one or two sizes bigger than usual because shrinkage occurs and the sizes tend to run smaller to fit the local build.

5. **Haggle.** Bargaining takes on a whole new meaning in China. It's more of a sport than a buying strategy, and it requires three things: preparation, a dispassionate attitude, and a clear head. Even if you're talking about only a few bucks, start your bargaining much lower and be prepared to walk out. You may get a better price. Of course, what you save on the price you may pay in the effort.

6. **Take a break.** A full day of bargaining for crap can be tiring. Every two hours or so, walk away and regroup. The shops and products aren't going anywhere.

7. **Set your max.** While most shops take credit cards, you should set aside the amount of money you are prepared to part with each

day. This way you can keep track of your daily spending and you won't be too shocked when the credit card bill comes.

8. **Just say no.** Don't be persuaded to buy something that you don't really want or will have no use for. Sounds easy enough, but quite a few times I walked away with a shirt in a color or style I didn't like. I don't know how it happened but it did—several times.

9. **Explore first.** If you walk into a marketplace that has a lot of shops, never buy from the one closest to the front door. It is often the most expensive shop and its vendors are the least willing to haggle.

10. **Go with your instinct.** If it seems too good to be true, it probably is. My computer-geek friend bought a "100-gigabyte flash drive" for $20. We were pretty sure that there was no such thing, even though the vendors demonstrated the device on their computer, but my friend bought it anyway. It was a total fake, didn't work, and ended up being a $20 piece of ugly keychain jewelry.

11. **Know when enough is enough.** How many lighters with Mao Zedong's picture does one actually need? Know when to call it quits.

12. **Declare it.** Customs and immigration agents aren't stupid. They know you have been to Asia, and they can see that stuffed duffel bag. Make a detailed list of your purchases daily, or at least as you are packing, and put it on your customs landing card.

The last purchase on my list was a purse that my wife had specifically requested. I had learned the art of haggling by then and considered myself something of a pro. I approached the vendor with a dispassionate attitude, pointed to the purse, and began what seemed like 45 minutes of hardcore haggling. The game was on. When I would pretend to walk away, the vendor would type a new number in her calculator. I would shake my head in disappointment and type in a much lower price. Eventually, I got her down to the bare minimum and we finished the deal with a handshake. With a frown she exclaimed, "Me lose money on this one."

I felt both guilty and proud as I handed over the money—until a local approached and bought the same exact item for approximately half of what I had paid. The vendor's frown turned to a smile and she winked as she said, "You come back tomorrow and I give you a better price."

The so-called pro had been demoted to novice in three seconds flat.

CHAPTER THIRTEEN

Lost in Kuwait

S ometimes I wake up with no recollection of where I am. The blinds are closed, the earplugs are in, and the hotel room looks just like every other hotel room. I go through the routine of re-tracing my steps and work it out after a few minutes. This particular morning, I woke up in Kuwait. I had flown in the night before, after working a military charter. Now that the war in Iraq has become a more permanent fixture, airline crews are ending up in Kuwait more often. I was on a five-day layover in a very foreign land.

The night before I left, I looked at the world map to see exactly where in the world I was off to. Kuwait is nestled in between Iraq and Saudi Arabia and lies across the Persian Gulf from Iran. It is an alcohol-free country, has temperatures that range between 60 and 130 degrees, and embraces many different cultures and beliefs. Luckily it was February, and the temperature held between 70 and 80 degrees. I had no intention of being cooped up in a hotel for five days and was eager to venture out and explore.

Kuwait is by no means a tourist destination, but why not treat it like one while I was there? My crewmates and I haggled at the Iranian marketplace, walked along the Persian Gulf, and ate cuisine ranging from Indian to Afghan. I love hummus, and since it is one of the region's specialties, I had it with every meal.

I now know what movie stars feel like in the public eye. We weren't harassed, but we were constantly stared at, even though we were observing the proper social etiquette, like not wearing shorts and showing no public affection between a man and a woman (ironically, affection between two men is considered fine and is frequently expressed). Other traditions are that women should cover as much of their skin as possible and walk behind the men. While this does not sit well with many in the United States, we weren't there to argue beliefs; we were there to experience and respect the ways of the world where we found ourselves.

We were staying in the capital, Kuwait City, where everyone was friendly. After Iraq invaded Kuwait in 1990, appreciation for America's involvement in the Middle East took hold here, and it is generally considered a pro-American country. Before long, I found a group of local people who had some basic English, and I picked up a few of their words and phrases.

From my new friends I learned that approximately 70 percent of the people living in Kuwait are from Iran, Iraq, Saudi Arabia, India, Qatar, and places beyond. It is a fascinating and remarkably vibrant mix of people. At sunset, prayer chants echoed throughout the city and wonderment filled my mind. I was in a new land, discovering a remote part of the world. I felt giddy, like a young traveler—the way I felt many years ago, when I started this flight attendant job.

On this trip I picked up a few tips that may help you make the best of your trip in any foreign destination:

1. **Avoid room service whenever possible.** It's costly, anti-social, and anti-cultural. It's just too easy, and it prevents you from getting out and seeing the real country.

2. **Respect and honor all local customs and cultural beliefs.** You are a guest, not a judge.

3. **Stay away from fast-food conveniences.** You can find a McDonald's just about everywhere in the world. But save the Big Mac for home. While you are in some exotic foreign land, go to an authentic local restaurant instead. (Curiously, KFC is very popular in Kuwait. After services at the mosques, the lines at this fast-food establishment are very long.)

4. **Don't be afraid to explore.** You are as interesting to the local people as they are to you. Be adventurous; some of the best experiences are unplanned or unexpected.

5. **Try to blend in a bit.** Don't broadcast the fact that you're a tourist. You won't get hassled as much if your attire doesn't scream "foreigner," and it's a lot safer.

6. **Raise a glass with the locals.** Unless you are in an alcohol-free country (as I was), ask the hotel concierge where the nice bars are. In Kuwait, I went to a local coffee house and smoked shisha (flavored tobacco) out of a hookah—a bagpipe-like contraption with hoses.

7. **Use the buddy system.** There is safety in numbers, and you should try to go out with at least one other person. Be safety conscious, but don't assume everyone is out to rip you off.

8. **Learn a little of the language.** Even if everyone understands English, the locals generally appreciate your effort.

9. **Look on the bright side.** Okay, so none of us could partake of alcoholic drinks for five days, and the crew party with blended smoothies was more boring than usual, but I felt great in the morning and slept better than ever.

10. **Enjoy yourself.** Don't be afraid to be a tourist—and don't be overly proud of it either. Instead, be yourself. Go on a tour. Take

pictures. Ask silly questions. It's nothing to be ashamed of. How many times are you going to visit this place in your lifetime?

Unfortunately, my crewmates and I were in Kuwait because of the war, but we managed to have a great time and learn a lot about a very different land. I got a new appreciation for my job, and I gained respect for the diversity of beliefs, customs, and peoples of the world.

CHAPTER FOURTEEN

Going, Abroad

The world's toilet facilities never cease to amaze me.

Consider the older women attendants in Germany, who have no problem mopping the floor as you do your business. Or the thoroughfare arrangement, in which female customers have to walk past the urinals to get to their toilet, as I've seen in Japan. And what about those coin dishes—does anyone know how much change to contribute? And let's not forget the famous hole in the ground, where the squat technique takes some getting used to. Other toilet surprises include pull-chain and infrared flushes, the "poo-with-a-view," and coed restrooms—not to mention wide variations in hygiene, condition, and smell.

Everyone has his worst traveling toilet story. Mine comes from Prague, where I paid the equivalent of a nickel to use the facility in the train station. The stench and the filth were so bad my eyes burned and I threw up instead. On my way out, I took back my nickel and yelled at the attendant, who seemed baffled by my reaction.

I've heard some pretty good stories, too—like getting caught behind the bushes, and squatting in an alley in front of a one-way window (a whole convention of people got a great back view). And then there was the female skier in the French Alps who dropped down her one-piece ski suit to squat behind a tree; her center of gravity shifted midstream, and she ended up skiing down the mountain, backwards, screaming the whole way. Can you imagine spotting that coming at you?

Sure, it's funny when it happens to someone else, but do you remember the last time you were in a foreign place, desperate to use the facilities, and there were none to be found? At that moment it's no laughing matter. This happens to me all the time, but after 20 years of international layovers, I consider myself something of an expert on this matter. So here are 10 tips and observations on the subject of "Going, abroad":

1. **Wipe out.** Always carry tissues or your own toilet paper. It only takes one instance of going without or using the sandpaper provided at some stalls to set you straight on this one.

2. **The change will do you good.** Always carry spare change in the local currency. The toilet facilities that you pay for are generally the most hygienic ones, except perhaps in Prague.

3. **McBathrooms.** In another chapter, I have criticized travelers for eating at McDonald's when abroad, but there's no denying that their restrooms can get you out of a pickle when you are abroad. If you have to order something to gain access, get a small bag of fries—it costs about the same as an attended toilet.

4. **Ooh, that smell!** If the odor is unbearable, put a wet wipe over your nose or put lotion on a tissue and use that to mask the smell.

5. **Squatter's rights.** It's daunting to enter a toilet and find a hole in the ground with two depressions for your feet, but after you get the hang of it, it feels quite natural, and apparently it's healthier as well. Ladies, skirts are easier to manage than trousers in such a place.

6. **Confidence counts.** Most every fancy hotel lobby has a restroom. Just walk in as if you are a guest. I have never been questioned or turned away.

7. **On the go.** Use the facilities whenever you get the chance. You may not have to go at the moment, but a little effort could save you from desperation hours later on the tour bus.

8. **Earplugs.** Readers of my books know that I think earplugs are the cure for just about everything and, yes, I have even worked them into bathroom advice. Personally, I can't stand some of the noises that emanate from the crowded stalls next to me. Apparently, I'm not alone. Did you know that many toilets in Japan produce running water when the user is seated, to mask all embarrassing sounds? Well, if you're not in Japan, try the earplugs. They will let you concentrate on the task at hand instead of flinching from the grunter next door.

9. **A no-go.** Know that if you risk going in public areas, like behind a tree or in an alley, you could be breaking the law, and the offense can carry fines or even jail time. A colleague of mine was so desperate to pee in London that he urinated against the House of Lords. He wound up in jail and had to plead no contest because he was caught with his fly down on video.

10. **Attitude adjustment**. It's all in the way you look at it. If you treat your trip to the toilet as a cultural lesson and a small adventure, you will come out of it with a smile.

I was once at a restaurant in Mexico and just barely touched a bowl of spices on the table before I went to the restroom. Let's just say I soon was on fire and in an unexpected place. For the longest time afterward, my airline nickname was "Jalapenis."

CHAPTER FIFTEEN

Lessons Learned In-Flight

I n the 18 years I have been flying, I think I have seen or heard just about everything, and yet, every flight can provide a valuable lesson. In school I was taught how to read and write, in sports I learned to play fair, and in the military I figured out how to take orders, but it wasn't until my flying career took off that I was educated about real life.

Here are some of my real-life lessons. They are inspired by Robert Fulguhm's wildly popular book. *All I Really Need to Know I Learned in Kindergarten,* except that in my case I learned everything on an airplane.

- **Wear your seat belt.**
- **Carry only what you can lift.**

- **Drink a lot of water,** even if you are not especially thirsty.

- **You always have an entrée choice**: to eat or not to eat.

- **Smile at people who annoy you.** It makes them nervous.

- **Talk to your seatmates.** You just might learn something. And if it turns out you don't like them, don't worry; you'll probably never see them again.

- **Always carry a good book with you.**

- **Never invest in airline stock**, especially if you work for the airline in question.

- **Duct tape fixes everything** (even airplane wings).

- **Don't get too caught up in the current hassle**, because the next one is just around the corner.

- **A watched conveyor belt doesn't bring your luggage quicker.**

- **Earplugs can make all the difference.**

- **Arrive early.** It will save your disposition, your composure, and your dignity. But if you don't arrive early, stop worrying. There is always another flight.

- **Say yes to know-it-alls.** Otherwise, they will just keep on talking.

- **Get up and stretch.**

- **Always have a back-up plan.**

- **Slow down!** You're missing the point of life.

- **Be sympathetic to your fellow traveler** (or employee). Lend him a hand when he needs it.

- **Take the window seat.** Middle seats just don't make sense.

- **When people ask what you do for a living, tell them you are a data processor.** No more questions will follow.

- **Always know where the nearest emergency exit is located.**

- **Put yourself in other people's shoes.** Try to understand what they are going through.

- **Don't envy the people in First Class.** They don't have half as much fun as the folks in Economy.
- **Tune out long-winded stories,** but have a general remark ready in case you are asked for an opinion.
- **If you don't think about the money you are spending on your trip, you will enjoy it more.**
- **Don't pack too much,** or you won't have room for souvenirs.
- **Life is a wonderful freak show,** and we all have front-row tickets.
- **Keep an open mind.**
- **Humor the people in charge.** Pilots may be full of hot air, but they get you where you're going safe and sound.
- **Create your own pension plan.** You never know when your company will run off with yours.
- **There is humor in just about everything,** so laugh at life's little annoyances. It's so much better than crying.
- **Red wine is good for you,** and white wine isn't so bad either.
- **Life is the journey,** not the destination.

About the Author

James Wysong (aka A. Frank Steward) has worked as a flight attendant with a major American international airline for 20 years. The author of *Air Travel Tales From the Flight Crew: The Plane Truth at 35,000 Feet* (2006), *The Plane Truth: Shift Happens at 35,000 Feet* (2004), and *Air Traveler's Survival Guide* (2002), James holds a bachelor's degree from a London university and has had a wide variety of jobs spanning continents: jazz trumpet player, bartender, appraiser, and MSNBC columnist. He currently writes a weekly column for www.tripso.com and www.MSNBC.com under his given name of James Wysong. His wife, who is also employed by the airlines, first as a flight attendant and now as a pilot, has recently upgraded to Captain. They live on the East Coast with their 2-year-old son Oliver.

Also Available
From James Wysong

The Plane Truth:
Shift Happens at 35,000 Feet

2003
ISBN 1-57023-211-3
$14.95

**Air Travel Tales
From the Flight Crew:**
The Plane Truth at 35,000 Feet

2005
ISBN 1-57023-242-3
$14.95

Keep in Touch . . .
On the Web!

www.impactpublications.com
www.ishoparoundtheworld.com
www.veteransworld.com
www.exoffenderreentry.com